FINANCIAL CENTS HOW TO SURVIVE IN A HIGH DOLLAR WORLD:

What Every Person Should Know AND Tell Their Children

By George R. Burke

Disclaimer:

The views and opinions expressed in this book are for the sole purpose of guiding people to make educated decisions about their financial affairs and how to save money, they are not written by a certified financial planner. In this book the author covers a wide range of experience from his own life and research. The author of this book does not carry any authority, credentials or certifications to give financial advice. Therefore, you are advised to consult a certified financial planner and/or tax consultant or other legal professional with any questions you have regarding any information found in this book, as well as any additional questions you may have in regards to managing your finances. The author will not be liable in any way for any losses from given advice. Further the author expressly suggests you research on your own, before you make any buying or investing decisions.

Copyright © 2012 George R. Burke

All rights reserved. No part of this publication may be reproduced, stored in a retrieval system or transmitted in any form or by any means electronic, mechanical, photocopying, recording or otherwise, without the prior written permission of the Author, except in the case of a reviewer, who may quote brief passages embodied in critical articles or in a review.

Printed in the United States of America

Table of Contents

Introduction – Be financially fit. Lower your monthly expenditures.

Make Saving Money Fun – Make it a game, a game that you win!

Avoid Long Term Debt – You don't know the future. Be prepared.

Make a Memory – Save money on bills. Put money in the bank & into life.

Hope for the Best, but plan for the Worst. – Life happens. We never know when.

Learn From Others Mistakes: You don't have to make mistakes, just learn lessons.

When Dealing With A Business – Don't be a number. Be a person.

Write It Down – The Old CYA – Make this a habit, starting today.

Establish A Budget: You can't change things unless you know what you started with.

Set Your Goals! – Short, medium and long term goals. Live your dreams.

What is credit?

Establishing and building cxredit

Maintaining credit - Why it is so important.

Destroy all personal information.

Credit Bureau information & resources

Auto Clubs & Roadside Assistance

AUTOMOBILES & VEHICLES

Choosing a vehicle.- What's important? Wants vs Needs
Look online to see what is available.

Buy cash if you can – Reduce your monthly debt.
Financing – What to keep in mind. Questions to ask?
Beware of financing tricks and add ons.

BANKS AND CREDIT UNIONS

Checking Accounts –
Save money and don't get burned.
Pay bills online
ATM fees
Save on check cashing & Money Order fees.
Visa/Master Card ATM Cards
Overdraft fees – Opt in or out
One last thing – If in doubt, ask for the manager!

FINANCIAL SERVICES

Warning! Do your research, before you invest.
Diversify
Tax implications and Capital Gains
Choosing an Investment Broker: Discount or Full Service
 401K's
Company Stock Options - .

CREDIT CARDS

How to get the most for your money!
Annual Fees
Interest
Payoff and Cash Check Offers – Cash costs more!
Points, Cash Back and Frequent Flyer Miles
Pay Off Your Highest Interest Credit Card First
If you have them, know what they can do for you.
Don't be taken advantage of – Fight Back!

REAL ESTATE

Sellers - Have a decision to make - To sell now or not to sell now?
Buyers - Get a good deal – Buy right!
Government Owned Foreclosure Websites

MORTGAGES

What is in a Mortgage Payment
Interest Only – Are there any benefits?
Adjustable Rate Mortgages
Fixed Rate Mortgage – 15 or 30 year term?
PMI - Private Mortgage Insurance – What is it & Can I get it removed?
3 Day Recision – When can you walk away from a bad loan?
Refinancing – Does it make sense?
Recasting – A possible option if you can't refinance.

INSURANCE

Try to combine policies if possible.
 Life Insurance – Try to cover your loved ones, if you can.
 1. Term Life Insurance
 2. Whole Life Insurance
Health Insurance
Discounted Prescription Drugs – Low cost alternatives
Automobile Insurance
Homeowners Insurance
Renters Insurance
Dwelling Policies
Flood Insurance

TAXES - THE TAX MAN COMETH.

Have the right amount of deductions taken out
File your Federal Taxes for free.

CABLE, SATTELITE OR ANTENNAE

Which is best for you?
Cable or Satellite Companies
Combine to save money!
Cable modems and equipment
High Speed Internet
Streaming video from the Internet

THE ELECTRIC & GAS COMPANIES

How can you save money?
Reducing your consumption.
Free Home Survey
Some of the best energy saving tips.

Low Income Home Energy Assistance Program (LIHEAP)
Free firewood and mulch.

WIRED, WIRELESS & INTERNET TELEPHONE

What works for you?
What kind of budget do you have?
How many phones will you need?
What if you lose your electric?
Be Careful to ask about data transfer limits.
Options and plans.
Go ahead make the change: Great offers can happen!
Security – 911 shows address, not with cell & Internet phones.
National Do Not Call List – Sign up to end the sales calls. Free!

CELL PHONES

Be careful, ask about Data Limits for wireless phones.
Are free cell phones & perks really free?
How to avoid "Bill Shock"

YOUR WATER BILL

When looking for a home – Look for one with a well.
Reducing water usage,
Reclaimed water. What if you do have a discrepancy?

LOCAL CITY GOVERNMENT

Freebies and help from your local community.
Police Department
Fire Department
Local Landfill
Government Owned and Seized Auction Website

COLLEGE CHOICES AND TUITION

In State College versus Out Of State College
Private College versus Public College
Federal Pell Grant Program
Have you considered a Rental Property?
Prepaid College Programs
Tax Benefits For Education

STORES AND GROCERY STORES

Go online to your local food stores website to see sale papers.
Coupons don't need to be extreme – Just save!
What's the best deal?
Call to find the stores coupon policy.
Find who offers double coupons and when.
Find out which store will price match.
Great deals on day old meats, bakery and produce.

YARD SALES, CONSIGNMENT SHOPS & CHARITIES = LOTS OF SAVINGS.

NEWSPAPERS

Nearly every newspaper has an online edition for free.
Sunday Paper – Coupons, Coupons, Coupons
Classified Ads

DISCOUNTED AIRLINE TICKETS

Why pay more than you have to.
Online – Discount travel sites.
Try combo packages.
Look at some of the small regional airlines.
Airline Websites.
If you have one of those Airline Miles Cards, use it.

HOTELS, MOTELS AND VACATION DESTINATIONS

Why would a hotel or motel offer a discount?
Online discount hotel websites.
Using your discounts.

TRAVELING AND ON THE ROAD TRIPS

Off the beaten path.
Special discounts and timeshares.
Local discounts.
Annual pass.
Reciprocal agreements.

INTRODUCTION

This book is loaded with straight talk on how to reduce your bills and overall debt. In addition, I have a significant amount of tips on some of the pitfalls to look for when signing up for a loan or long term debt. I have also included some of the best things that our family has used to save money and live in today's expensive society on one income.

One of the things that that we lack in the teaching of our young people in today's society is how to get the most from your money and how to be financially fit. We all hear every day on television or in the magazines how important fitness is to our overall health and well-being, but every single person out there also needs to pay attention to their financial well-being as well. I have always told my children, "If you can save money on the things that you NEED to purchase, such as your household bills and expenses, than that leaves more for what you WANT to buy, or to put some in the bank for a rainy day." You never know what is coming in your future. It's a fine line to decide what to do with the money that you save, but that is for later in this book.

The author in his extensive sales career (35 years and counting), at various times has been a: Loan Officer, Automobile Sales and Finance person, Florida Life and Health Insurance Agent, Notary, Florida Real Estate Agent, missed his Florida Mortgage Broker License by one point after only reading the book. No classroom study. My point in telling you this is not to blow my own horn, but to tell you that I have been heavily involved, behind the scenes, in various forms of negotiations, finance and contractual obligations throughout my career and my life. In this book, I try to bring some information out to the reader and possible scenarios to consider. It's not necessarily fun reading but it is very important reading. You will learn a great deal.

When making any large decision it is always best to research before you sign the papers and get everything in writing. Make your own mind up what is best for you, but this may give you some basic understanding of the steps that are involved and some resources as we get into the nuts and bolts of this book to start you along the path of resources.

The internet is an amazing force in today's society. Many times I have wished back twenty or thirty years ago that I had the vast amount of resource material and information out there, but always be wary. Make sure you use reputable sites. There is a lot of biased and misinformation spread around on the internet also. Don't be misled.

MAKE SAVING MONEY FUN
MAKE IT A GAME, A GAME THAT YOU WIN!

Make it a game and see how much you can save using the tips from this book as a starting point. See how far you can stretch your money. You will be amazed if you take this to heart. Every time you save money, think to yourself or tell someone you love how much you saved for the family. They may begin to play the game also and you could have the whole family benefiting from saving money on things that many people don't even think about or know these discounts are even available. They might only complain about the charges AND PAY THEM.

If you purchased this book you have taken the first step to financial freedom! You will probably save hundreds if not thousands of dollars a year if you take all these tips to heart. If you have any great tips of your own that you would like to share, please let me know at **georgerburke@yahoo.com** so that I can filter through and share with other readers in subsequent updates to this book for all to benefit from.

AVOID LONG TERM DEBT

One of the best things to remember is, don't limit yourself if at all possible. In this instance I am talking long term debt. I know that the ultimate goal for many people is to own their own home and this is something that we all need to pay in monthly payments but I am talking about long term commitments to cable companies, satellite companies, cell phone carriers, etc. These are all long term commitments. You might have a great paying job and easily be able to make these payments when you start these plans. You think this will always be the case, but you could lose that job or be forced to move to another area. You may have to help with an elderly family member. My point, who knows what will be going on in your life a year or two down the road? What if all of a sudden you lost your income and you are facing these large monthly payments. Where is the money going to come from? Even if you call and cancel the plans and don't need to have that service anymore, there are probably hundreds of dollars in penalties that will be due on each you are forced to cancel. Always make it a goal to pay as you go, if possible, and look to tie yourself up for the least amount of time possible on the things that you feel you want in your life.

MAKE A MEMORY

I will never forget a sad but inspiring story I was told once. I was working as a loan officer early in my sales career (I hated that job). I would be there ready to close up the office and like clockwork, every month an older woman would bring in her payment on a loan that she had taken out. I would process her payment and give her a receipt. We would be talking normal small talk. Well one day, she seemed a little down. I had been talking to her every time she came in to the office to make her payment. I asked her how things were going. I mentioned that she looked a little down and asked if she was OK? She slowly opened up and began to tell me her story, with tears in her eyes.

She said that she and her husband had been doing all of the right things throughout their marriage. The gold ring at the end of the rainbow, for them, had been to travel when they retired. They worked diligently, scraping up every penny they could and squirreled it away into a savings account for their golden days of retirement. Her husband had worked for a company some twenty five years or so and was due a good pension. As their retirement approached, they felt that they were prepared for a wonderful time in their Golden Years. All of their preparations were in place.

When her husband retired from his long career at 65 years old they were ecstatic. They took out a loan, to purchase an RV. They wanted to follow their dreams to travel the country. They had it all, money in the bank, he had a good retirement pension they could count on and he was now getting Social Security.

Well, they sold their home and their belongings and put the money in the bank and hit the road. They thoroughly enjoyed themselves for about a year when his former company, that he was getting his well-deserved pension from, after 25 years of service, was purchased by another company and they ended pension plans. They changed the rules on him after he had nothing to give. In one fell swoop, they lost more than fifty percent of their income.

Life on the road is not cheap, you have gas for the RV and then you have to pay to stay in the RV parks, which can add up to hundreds of dollars a month plus food and anything else that you would normally pay for. Bottom line, after losing a large part of his income, the stress fell on them both to make up the shortfall from their savings. With all the stress taking its toll, the husband had a heart attack after another six months, While he survived the heart attack, the medical bills ate up nearly everything they had in savings within a year and a half. They were back to trying to live on Social Security and with his medical condition, after the heart attack, he was unable to travel anymore. They had to go back to renting a house since they had sold their home and put everything into the bank.

I felt so sorry for these folks. I will never forget the woman's words to me. She said "Son, don't do like we did, putting everything away for the future that may not come. Make a memory. If you have an extra thirty dollars, put ten of it away for when needs arise. Life happens. But take that other twenty dollars and make a memory with your wife and kids. Now with all of our money gone and my husband's health being what it is, all I have are my memories, and I have so few of them. I so wish we would have been making the memories all along. Then I would have a long and fulfilled life. I feel we lost out on so much and I feel cheated. Don't let that happen to you"

From that day until this I have tried to heed her advice. I have made memories and tried to save as much on what we have to spend money on in life so that we can use that money to either make memories or put some away for a rainy day. It's a delicate balance, but all of life is. There are always choices to be made in any situation. If you put together a game plan, you can indeed "have your cake and eat it too" as they say.

"HOPE FOR THE BEST, BUT PLAN FOR THE WORST."

Life Happens. Make a game plan and be as prepared as you can. It's not thinking negatively to be prepared. It's smart. In the event that something happens that causes you to spend more than you make in a month. It might be a transmission that falls out of your car while driving, or losing your job, which happens so often in these tough times. When you are working, put some money away. Start squirreling away whatever you can. Not everything mind you, but take a little bit each week or each paycheck and put it into a bank or some safe place. Start out small but START TODAY.

Don't put it off. You will be amazed at how quickly that money will grow and you won't even miss it. It also reduces your stress level, to know that you have a little money in the bank…IF.

LEARN FROM OTHER'S MISTAKES!

One other thing you should remember. Learn from other people's mistakes. It's not a nice thing to say, but look around you. I am sure that we all have seen friends and family members make a life changing mistake that they had to pay for dearly.

One of my daughter's friends came home to her parents, pregnant at 14 years old. I was heartbroken, not for the beautiful baby that was inside her. It is hard to look into the bright eyes of a baby that has been born into this world and think they are a mistake. They are truly a gift from God. I just had wished that she had waited until she was more secure in this world, to have that little gift from God.

Despite what people say, kids are not raised on love alone. They take money and lots of effort, work AND love. There are constant feedings, changings, crying at night, doctor appointments and daycare. Someone babysitting is the only way to get any free time at all. This girl I knew was going to have a very hard life and unfortunately her decision threw the parents into an unfortunate situation as well. They did not have any choice in this matter, not any real choice anyway. The only choice they had was either to deal with the situation and take a lot of the stress and pressure on themselves, whether they liked it or not, or to throw the daughter and new grandchild out on the street. Obviously the later was not a choice that was easily considered, and was quickly eliminated.

Here was a beautiful, young girl who was not even legally able to get a job in most states, or drive. How could she get a place of her own, get to the grocery store, stay in school, have a job, pay for daycare expenses. She just plain couldn't. She was still a child herself. I just knew how HARD her life was going to be and she and her boyfriend had brought this upon themselves. I could only hope for the best for them. I did however, tell my daughter to think seriously of all of these things that I have brought up and to think about what it would be to be in this young girl's position. The days of playing Barbie's were over for this young girl. The carefree days of playing house and being a real mom had happened overnight. It was very stressful and quick.

The point from all of this is, if you see the hardships or mistakes that someone in your life has brought onto themselves by the choices that they have made, take it as a learning lesson and try to put yourself in that person's shoes for a moment. It may help you deal with that person a little better, if you see them tired or stressed or if they seem a little different than they have always been. Maybe you can understand a little more what they are going through, but equally as important, learn from their mistake. Take it upon yourself not to take the same steps that has placed them in this predicament so that you do not have to pay those same consequences. These can be both financial lessons but can also be life lessons as well. Every one of us has made a mistake that others could have learned from in our lives. We may not yell it from the roof tops. We might not want anyone to know the mistakes we have made, but believe me, we are all human.

WHEN DEALING WITH A BUSINESS DON'T BE A NUMBER, BE A PERSON.

Be nice to people, whether it's the clerk behind the counter or the manager. Let them see you as a hard working individual, concerned about your money and making it last. Remember, all of these people, when they walk out of their workplace, are consumers also. Many, if not all, have the exact same needs and wants for themselves and their families that you do. Connect with these people as a person, so they can see you as more than just a spreadsheet or a page on their computer screen. Learn their names and use their name. Deal with them in a pleasant manner every time that you see them. Don't be demanding and abrupt. If they are able to help you or save you some money, let them know how much it means to you and that you appreciate it.

If Linda is into cooking and you know of a great recipe, share it with her. If you went out to a nice Chinese restaurant, maybe ask her if she likes Chinese food and share with her the place you went if it was good. Look for things that you have in common with the people that you meet. Remember them and your conversations of commonality. If a bank manager is nice to you and you meet someone that is looking for a great bank, share with them your experience. The next time you see the Bank Manager let them know that you referred them a customer. They will appreciate that in return. The old adage, "You will get more with Sugar than Vinegar" is true.

WRITE IT DOWN: MAKE THIS A HABIT, START TODAY.

That's right. The Old CYA (Cover you're a**). Listen, everyone makes mistakes. It's a fact of life, both you as an individual and also those that are in business. In addition you may need information if you happen to deal with a business that is not above board to prove what you are saying, if it comes to your word against theirs. This could come up say, if you are making a complaint to a Federal Regulatory Agency overseeing a group of businesses such as Building Contractors, Banks, Real Estate Agents, Mortgage Brokers, Doctors, Lawyers and others. It could also be important if you have to take a business to small claims court. Luckily this occurs rarely, but you may need to fill in the blanks even with a reasonable business. Remember, Managers need good information to make good decisions. Without good information, they can only rely on what they have internally on their computers or in talking to their own people. They will rely, nine times out of ten, on their own internal information without sticking their head out, so you need to fill in any good and credible information that might be missing so they can get a complete picture.

As an example: Sometime you may talk to someone about a problem with your phone bill and say Stephanie says she will give you a credit for the amount in question. Well a month goes by, and you get the same bill in the mail and you call the phone company back. Let's say that Stephanie was let go from the company and did not make the notes on your account. Maybe she still works for the company but cannot recollect the conversation. Which do you think would be better and more believable, If you said to her or her manger that you called "April 29, 2012 and spoke with Stephanie and faxed her the information requested to 800-***-**** and that she had said she would have the $29.00 credited or if you said I talked to a lady last month, and faxed her something and she said she was going to have that $29.00 credited. That makes a world of difference in your case if you keep detailed notes including names, phone numbers, extensions, dates and the outcome of the call. You are giving credible information. This is very helpful if you are dealing with government agencies for long drawn out processes when applying for say things like Social Security, Disability, Food Stamps (SNAP) to name a few. Many times multiple phone calls are needed and I would try to keep copies of any paperwork submitted to them, in case they misplace what you faxed or mailed them previously. If you do this, you don't have to research the information all over again and start all over from square one.

Many government agencies are renowned for asking for multiple copies of the same information. You need it when it is requested and will help them also if it has been misplaced. Many people have to touch the same file in these situations that take so much time.

ESTABLISH A BUDGET

What's a budget? A budget is a financial plan that takes into effect all of the money that you take in and all that you spend. It includes saving, borrowing and spending. You can't change things unless you know what you started with. It is the starting point and the game plan that you put into place to achieve the goals that you want. Your goal could be to get six months expenses into your bank account, in case you lost your job. It could be money to buy a car or to save for a down payment for a house. You set the goal, whatever they may be and you work hard either by yourself or as a couple (if married or in a relationship) to achieve.

To establish a budget, first figure out all streams of income you have coming into your home and mark them down on paper. It is much easier to visualize when things are written down. Then figure out all of the monthly bills that you have to pay, rent, mortgage payments, auto loan payments, electric, water, phone, insurances, food, etc. Once you have these bills figured out, hopefully when you take a combined total of your income, and subtract the total of your expenses you will have money left over. This money left over is called expendable income. This expendable income is what you want to increase as much as possible. It is what gives you the spending money to make memories, to do things that you want to do or to put some away into savings to reach a goal that you want to achieve like we discussed earlier. The key to a good financial life is to REDUCE your monthly bills, to as low as possible and to INCREASE your expendable income, as much as possible. The lower the amount you have to spend every month on bills, the more money you will have for the things in life that you really want. Now you are ready for the next step.

SET YOUR GOALS!

Now you are ready to set your goals. You should have a series of goals: short term goals, medium term goals, and long term goals. Be realistic when you set any type of goal. If you are afraid of heights, don't set a goal to become an Astronaut. There is an old saying: "A goal without a plan is just a wish." You can empower yourself to achieve your dreams, by setting goals. Set the goal for yourself. Think hard about it, what would be needed to achieve this dream. What steps do you need to take to reach that dream. Once you have taken your dream and added a plan to reach it and achieve that dream, then it becomes a goal. Goals are achievable. Start taking those steps today. It's like they say "Baby Steps". You don't have to make large steps each day, but always try to move yourself forward. Look to take opportunity's that arise in life to point yourself in the right direction, so that eventually you will achieve the goal and ultimately to LIVE THE DREAM, LIVE YOUR DREAM.

EXAMPLES OF SHORT TERM GOALS – Things that you might achieve in a few hours or maybe a day to achieve. These should be easy to accomplish, if you set your mind to it. These are things that, as you achieve your goals, should help you increase your own self-worth (be proud of yourself, feel good about yourself) and also will get you into the routine of having positive outcomes in your life.

- Check into finding local flying schools and costs involved.
- Check into costs & information on Web Hosting building a web site.
- .Look at the bills that you pay monthly, look for waste or things you don't need.

EXAMPLES OF MEDIUM TERM GOALS – Things that you might achieve in few days or a few weeks. These should be multiple task oriented goals, to get you on your road to your future. They are steps that lead toward your ultimate goal..

- Start taking flying lessons.
- Create and build a working Web Site.
- Contact one of the company's you pay monthly to see how you can save money

EXAMPLES OF LONG TERM GOALS - Things that you might achieve in from one to five years down the road. These goals take a lot of work but once accomplished these are those ultimate goals that place you in your own future.

- Pass your Pilot's License test and become a pilot.
- Turn your online Web Site into a money making business.

- Reduce your monthly bills to the lowest possible amount.

WHAT IS CREDIT?

Simply put Credit is anything that you borrow. To obtain goods or services before you have paid for them. There are two things that a lender looks at before giving you credit. It is nearly impossible to get credit without both of the conditions below:

1.) The intention to repay the loan or note.
2.) The ability to repay the loan or note.

THE INTENTION TO REPAY THE LOAN - is why people or institutions that are looking to lend you money or finance a car or mortgage, pull your credit history. The idea being, if you handled your other bills and paid them back to the terms of your agreement, then you will probably pay this one back also. If you have blown off your previous creditors and did not pay them back or they went to collections, then it is not likely that this lender will allow you to borrow the money that you need, because they are taking a greater risk at losing their money.

Some businesses are willing to take that risk but you will pay a much higher rate of return for the extra risk that they are taking in lending you the money. Sometimes you may need those types of loans but be VERY WARY and read and understand everything before you sign for any loan. In addition, get everything IN WRITING. I see all these commercials on TV with smiling people taking out Payday Loans or in particular Title Loans. Make sure that you fully understand what percentage rate you are paying (the amount of money you have to pay back) and when your payments are due. With many Title Loans if you miss payments, they may repossess your car. Imagine how hard life would be without your car, than think very hard to see if you really want to borrow that money. Sometimes it may be that important, but know what you are signing up for and be sure that you know how much you need to pay and how much each payment will be. Make sure that you have the necessary means to pay that loan back or your life could be in a world of hurt, not only your financial life but your regular life.

THE ABILITY TO REPAY YOUR LOAN – is your job or what income you have coming in. They will look at the bills you pay out and compare to your income (the amount of money you make.) They will see if you have the expendable income or money left over after all your bills are paid to repay this new loan.

ESTABLISHING & BUILDING CREDIT

I will give you an example of a credit situation that happened to a young man from my past. He was about 21 and just left college. He had been living with a roommate. They had an apartment in a decent apartment complex in Virginia. They decided to move to Florida. When they had first moved into the apartment complex, they had been charged first month's rent, last month's rent and a security deposit which equaled one month's rent. They did not know where they were going to move in Florida (no forwarding address) as they wanted to go down and check things out to find a place. Being young and not having a forwarding address to have the Security Deposit returned and not wanting to deal with the hassle, they decided to not pay the last month's rent and leave the security deposit as their last month's rent. They figured they would leave the key in the afterhours drop box at the office and all would be even. Well they loaded up the truck, did the dishes and vacuumed the place and did just that. The young man and his roommate moved to Florida to get on with their lives. About three years later when the man was 24 he went to get a car loan. He had never had credit of any kind to this point in his life. The car dealer ran his credit report and he was denied the car loan for delinquent credit. Well the guy knew that he had never had any credit and by law asked for and received a copy of his credit report. The only thing listed on his report was an apartment complex in Maryland (a state he had never lived in). There was a balance of about $150 that was listed on the report as an I9. On a credit report at the time an I on the report indicated it was an installment loan (a set monthly payment for a certain period of time), an R would have indicated a revolving loan (like a credit card where the balance can go up and down). The 9 indicated that the debt had gone to collections and eventually been written off as an unrecoverable debt. He called the 800 number to dispute the claim by the creditor and found out the story.

This apartment complex in Maryland was the parent company of the one he had lived in, years earlier, in Virginia. It seems that when he left the apartment, they had charged him a $50 cleaning fee of the apartment as was their policy and since they had no forwarding address to send the bill they charged $100 additional for attorney's fees and had it placed on his credit report. Well the young man realized that it was indeed a debt that he was responsible for and he asked the woman on the phone, if he were to pay off the $150 amount if they would take it off of his credit report as it was messing him up. She readily agreed. This is where he made his mistake. He should have gotten the agreement in writing. A man of his word, he went and had a bank check made out and sent it to them. The check was cashed and he went to try and get a car loan again. He was denied for the same reason. When he received a copy of this credit report this time, he found that the company had not been true to their word. They had written the balance down to zero but had left the I9 on his credit report. This is where it would have been helpful to have this in writing before he paid off the loan. In essence the company had written of the debt and received a tax credit for the loss, then had been paid the money, years later, which they received as income. They had in essence gotten $300 credit for the $150 dollar debt and screwed the young man over leaving it on his credit history. That goes to show you. First try to keep all of your credit positive so you're not in the situation but if you find yourself in a collection situation, ALWAYS GET IN WRITING WHAT YOU EXPECT, IF YOU PAY OFF THE DEBT, AND THE AMOUNT AGREED UPON.

To start out with credit START SMALL. Make sure that what you borrow, you can pay back. You may have to ask mom and dad to co-sign for the loan or credit card. Don't destroy your parent's hard earned credit rating by not paying the bills on time. As a co-signer that person is taking a great deal of risk and they are showing how much you mean to them. By co-signing for a loan or credit card they are telling the creditor, if their son/daughter does not pay the loan in the agreed upon times and amounts, than the burden falls on the cosignor to pay off the loan. Understand this, if you screw up and don't pay the payments like you should. If your late or don't pay the loan back you are going to hurt the person that was willing to help you when you needed it the most. You might mess up 30 years of great credit for mom and dad by just not bothering to pay for what you agreed.

MAINTAINING CREDIT: WHY IT IS SO IMPORTANT.

Credit is extremely important in life. It may be something as simple as having someone let you borrow their chain saw. If you return that chainsaw in a timely manner after using it and its gassed up and cleaned and in as good of condition as you borrowed, then that person will probably be happy to lend it to you again.

If you have that chain saw for two months and they have to track you down to get their own chain saw back (which is an inconvenience) when they need it and the equipment is messed up or out of gas, guess what? You probably will not be able to borrow that chainsaw again from that person (or anything else for that matter). Sounds like common sense, right? Well not as many people are endowed with common sense as you might think. Some have to learn the correct way to handle this kind of a situation.

We are all faced many times in our lives where we ask to borrow something. In the situation above we saved ourselves from going out and buying something for $150 or more that we would only need one time. In other situations, where we have to purchase things that cost much more money than we have, the only way to get those items is to get someone or a business to give you credit, where you can pay them back in payments over time. These are larger situations such as buying a car or a house, college tuition, or maybe even if the kids need braces, etc. Those situations call for us to try and get a loan. It is far easier to get a loan of this magnitude if the company can see how you have handled your credit before. That is why the lenders pull up your credit history. That is also why it is some important to show some credit history, something that you have paid in a timely basis, and paid off per your agreement.

In the instances of a car or a house, the lenders will have a secured loan. What this means is they will have a note which is the agreement for you to pay back the loan (X amount per month X the amount of months or years that you need to make the payments) but understand they are secured by what is called collateral. Collateral means something of value that you are putting up, saying to the lender, if I don't pay you the payments, you may take my car or house to help offset your loss. That is their security that you will actually pay for the item.

In an unsecured loan, they are really looking at you to do what you say. It's like a hand shake. You are saying, I will do this, and it's important to keep your word to that person or lender. They are taking a lot of risk with you if you have no track record. For this reason you want to build a credit history by taking on small debts when they arise and paying them off in the agreed upon monthly payments or even better, pay them off early if you can.

I once had a bank manager tell me to take an unsecured loan out. I asked him what the minimum Certificate Of Deposit (CD for short) they offered at the bank. This is basically a savings account that you need to leave in the bank for a period of time, usually six months or a year or longer. The longer that you leave the money in the bank, the more interest you earn. Well the bank manager told me the minimum amount of CD was $1500. I asked him what the minimum unsecured line of credit (sometimes called a signature loan) was. He told me $1500. I proposed to him that I did not have any credit but had a good job, I asked him if he would give me the $1500 loan and take the money and put it in a Certificate of Deposit in my name but keep it in his vault where he knew that the money was secure. Then I would give him a payment in advance right now. He agreed. He would be crazy not to. Banks are in the business to make money. I was borrowing $1500 and depositing $1500 in his bank plus was giving him a payment in advance that was just pure profit if the loan went bad, which of course I had no intention of it doing. He suggested to me, to increase my credit rating even better, to double up on the payments but not pay off the entire amount until at least six months went by.

The reason to not pay it off in less than six months was to make sure it was to make sure it actually was reported by the bank on my credit. If I were to pay the loan off too early, then the bank may have not have the time to report my payment history to the Credit Bureaus. The best credit that you can have is to pay your loan back earlier than agreed upon. I did exactly that and never looked back.

DESTROY PERSONAL INFORMATION

WORD OF WARNING – When you have to get rid of things like Bank Checks that have been sent to you through the mail or credit card offers that say pre-approved and old bank statements or stuff that has your personal information on them, always destroy these papers. Burn them, shred them and place in separate garbage bags, never the same one. Do not ever under any circumstances throw them in the trash for God knows who to find in the dump or blowing around on your street. Good Credit is way too hard to come by. It takes hard work and effort to build a sound credit history. Don't throw it all away, literally.

I keep an envelope with anything like this that I use in our fireplace to start our fires. I burn all personal information. Here is another word to the wise. DON'T EVER GIVE OUT YOUR PERSONAL INFORMATION OVER THE PHONE SUCH AS YOUR SOCIAL SECURITY NUMBER OR DATE OF BIRTH. Call them back after checking them out. If someone calls you and says they are from your bank and need to verify some information, ask them for a number where you can reach them. Check and verify that this number is actually your banks number and then call back to ask for the individual. Do not ever offer information to someone over the phone. If it is someone trying to rip you off it's a numbers game, more than likely they will move on and give you a bad number. In today's day and age even with caller ID it can be circumvented in some situations.

CREDIT BUREAU INFORMATION

By law you can pull your credit bureau report to see what companies are reporting on you once per year. In addition, if you are denied credit for any reason you can file within thirty days to get a free copy of the report telling you why you were denied credit. There are quite a few places out there to pull a credit report. Many of these are trying to sell you something. The one listed on U.S. Government website USA.gov is the link below. It links to all three credit reporting agencies at one time.

https://www.annualcreditreport.com/cra/index.jsp

Once you pull your credit report if you see something that is not you or if there is an error you have the right to dispute something that appears on the report if it is incorrect. Remember there are a lot of people out there with the same name or even when someone at the Credit Bureau may be typing in a Social Security Number for instance, they may input one wrong digit and it could come up as your Social Security Number. Here is a link on how to dispute something on your Credit Bureau Report:

http://www.ftc.gov/bcp/edu/pubs/consumer/credit/cre21.shtm

The information in your credit report is used to calculate your FICO (the acronym stands for Fair, Isaac and Company) score. Your score can range anywhere from 300-850.. Aiming for a score in the 700s will put you in good standing. A high score, for example, makes it easier for you to obtain a loan, rent an apartment, or lower your insurance rate. Your FICO score is available for a fee. Free credit reports do not contain your credit score, although you can purchase it when you request your free annual credit report.

To find out more about your FICO Credit Score and how they come up with your number here is the link:

http://www.myfico.com/CreditEducation/WhatsInYourScore.aspx

The three main Credit Bureaus or Credit Reporting Agencies and their contact information are listed below:

Experian
P.O. Box 9556
Allen, TX 75013

Office in TX: 1-888-397-3742
Business: 1-888-211-0728
Fraud Hotline: 1-888-397-3742

WEB SITE: http://www.experian.com/index-bu.html

Equifax
P.O. Box 740241
Atlanta, GA 30374-0241

Business Line (also has option for Personal): 1-888-202-4025
Office in GA: 1-800-685-1111
Dispute Fax #: 1-888-826-0573
Business: 1-802-304-0364
General: 1-800-797-6801
Fraud Hotline: 1-888-766-0008

WEB SITE: http://www.equifax.com/home/en_us

TransUnion
Trans Union Consumer Relations
P.O. Box 2000
Chester, PA 19022-2000

Office in PA: 1-800-888-4213
1-888-259-6845
1-800-916-8800 (consumer relations)
Fraud Hotline: 1-800-680-7289

WEB SITE: http://www.transunion.com/

AUTO CLUBS AND ROADSIDE ASSISTANCE

We have all heard horror stories of someone breaking down on a lonely stretch of road and calling a towing service who comes out to help, only to find out that they want hundreds of dollars in CASH to get you back to civilization or to tow you to the nearest service station.

For anyone who travels the roads on a regular basis, you should know that being a member of a good auto club is a great way to save money and have peace of mind for you and your family. Whether your car breaks down and needs towing or your battery goes dead and you need a jump start, it's good to have help a simple phone call away. For as little as $60 to $70 a year, you can have coverage for a variety of different issues that arise. Some Auto Clubs are able to get you discounts on everything from hotels to insurance and offer a variety of services included with your membership that could easily pay for itself. You never know when something might go wrong, but its nice to know that if something does happen it won't cost you an arm and a leg. I add my grown children to my membership at a discounted rate as a Christmas present and I know I am helping them all year around.

A couple of the most well-known Auto Clubs are listed below to start your research.

American Automobile Association

http://www.aaa.com

Good Sam Roadside Assistance

http://www.goodsamers.com/auto/

AUTOMOBILES & VEHICLES

CHOOSING A VEHICLE

So you are buying a different vehicle are you, is it better to buy new or used? That is the question. Let me tell you a few things to keep in mind. What is important to you? We are all different. Ask yourself two questions. What do I NEED to have in this car or vehicle? This might be considering that you need an automatic transmission because you don't know how to drive a manual transmission (stick shift) vehicle. You probably need to have a vehicle that won't break down on you all the time. Maybe you should do some research online before you even go out looking for a vehicle, to find what other people say about the type of auto or truck that you are considering. The needs are very basic. Does it have the room that you need?

Is it powerful enough to tow something if that is required? Is this car generally considered dependable? Will the insurance be affordable? Maybe you have small children and a station wagon or at least a four door vehicle is important so that you can easily get the kids in the car seats. A vehicle needs to transport you and your friends/family to work or school and should be dependable because you will be relying on this vehicle to get you where you need to go in your life's calling.

The next question is: What would I WANT to have in the vehicle that I am buying? That is important because if you are going to be paying a lot of money out to buy a different vehicle than you want to be happy with your choice. But keep this in mind. These things are not needs. Maybe you would like a kicking stereo system or maybe you really have a particular color of car that you wanted. These are things that you would prefer to have if you had the choice but would not be deal breakers.

LOOK ONLINE TO SEE WHAT IS AVAILABLE.

Once you have decided what type of vehicle you are interested in purchasing you should start by doing a little research before you go out looking for it. The internet is a wonderful thing. I wish it had been available when I first started out (before Former Vice President Al Gore Invented It…hehehe). Some of the things you might be interested in checking out are in the following links:

NATIONAL AUTO DEALERS ASSOCIATION (NADA) - Valuation – To find out what average retail and trade in values for cars, trucks, vans, boats and RV's you can go to their web site,. It is very easy to use and will give you a pretty good idea of what the value of a vehicle that you are buying or selling will be either as a trade in or retail.

http://www.nadaguides.com/

KELLEY BLUE BOOK – Another great tool to compare pricing on a vehicle – new or used, that you are looking to either purchase or sell. The Kelley Blue Book has been around since 1926 and is loaded with valuable information free of charge.

http://www.kbb.com.

CRAIGSLIST – Is an excellent online website where Individuals and dealers sell vehicles as well as many other items. BUYER BEWARE! – Take precautions when meeting anyone with cash. Just be smart. I would always let someone know I will come out to check the vehicle out and then if we come to an agreement, I would ask them to follow me to my local bank to complete the transaction so I am not carrying cash.

www.craigslist.org

PAY CASH IF YOU CAN

Cars are generally an asset that depreciates in value. This means they go down in value as they get older (not all vehicles). We have all heard about people purchasing a new car and BEING UPSIDE DOWN. What that term actually means, is that you owe more money than your car is worth. That is never a good situation to be in. Why would you want to pay more for something than it's worth? Would you go to the grocery store and buy a gallon of milk that has a price of $5.00 on the shelf and when you get to the register say, I will give you $6.00 for that gallon of milk. No of course not. Well try your best to avoid this when buying a different vehicle also.

Remember, the ultimate goal financially is to reduce your monthly debt, or what you pay on a monthly basis. This in turn reduces your overall debt (what you owe). So that being said, I have always asked myself, if I can buy a car for say $1500 cash and it lasts 3 years, that that's better than paying $300 a month which would be $10,800 (3 years = 36 months X $300 = $10,800). So the point is, try to buy something that you can afford cash if possible. This would also include any trade in that would count towards the cash price. This is always the best for your monthly budget. Sure there may be some things that need to be fixed or replaced on a used vehicle, but those expenses should still be far less than the monthly payments total out to be.

FINANCING

Now, not everyone has an extra few thousand available. That is understandable. That is exactly why you would have been building your credit score up. First find a car that suits your needs, whatever they may be. Than call your insurance company to see how much your insurance would be for that vehicle. Most if not all states require that you carry insurance on your car and you want to be able to make sure BEFORE YOU BUY that you will be able to handle both the automobile payment AND the insurance payment. Once you find the insurance cost and you can afford it, check with the car dealership what kind of financing they can offer you and at what interest rate. Obviously the lower your annual percentage rate, the lower amount you are paying to borrow the money to purchase the vehicle. VERY IMPORTANT: You should ask the auto dealer if they report to the credit bureaus. This is important in your need to build a good credit history.

If you have to finance a vehicle, then it is best to have it show up on your credit history. Car loans generally have higher dollar amounts of credit and larger monthly payments then credit cards and if you pay these monthly payments per your agreement that you should get the benefits of a good credit history because of all your hard work.

Now, if you have a good relationship with your bank, call them and see if you can get better terms or lower interest rates. Does your work allow you access to a Credit Union that you can go through to get the loan. Are you a member of a Credit Union? Credit Unions many times have the best rates available if you can get a loan through them. They usually only offer the loans if you are a member. You may want to check into joining one if it makes sense.

A couple of things you also may want to consider. Obviously monthly payments are important, but what you really need to do is look at the payment and the term combined. If you find that one place is offering you $300 a month and another is offering you $250 a month for the same vehicle. Which is better, the $250 a month one right? Well let's see. We really don't have enough information to make that decision. What if the $300 is for 2 years (24 Months X $300 = $7200) and the $250 a month is for 3 years (36 months X 4250 = $9000). If you can afford the $300, then you will actually save $1800. Man, that $1800 is better off in your pocket, than it is in someone else's. You can make a lot of memories on $1000 and put the $800 in savings. You get the idea.

BEWARE OF FINANCING TRICKS & ADD ONS

The next thing about financing you should be aware of. Some finance managers will ask you the question. How much can you afford? Sounds like they are looking out for your best interest right? Well maybe they are, BUT if you give a monthly payment to them, they may add in any number of things into the paperwork. Things such as extended warranties, undercoating (rust protection- sprayed on underneath the car) of even Credit Insurance (Long Term Life and Disability Insurance's). Now understand, there are instances where all of these may be something that you want, but you should be aware that you are purchasing them. The first reason you should know, is to understand that these are large amounts of money, built into the loan that you are paying interest on over the whole time-period that you are paying off the loan.

Classically many places will add some or all of these or other things into your loan and extend the loan out for more years to give you a lower payment which everyone wants. This is why I gave you the previous example. The only way to really find out what is the better deal is to look at the payment and also the length of the loan as well as itemized paperwork showing what exactly you are paying for and what it will cost you to borrow the money. After all things are considered, you may find that you may not need these items or you may be able to find them for less money elsewhere, if you paid cash.

The second reason that you should be aware of these items built into your loan is if you actually need them, you want to be able to use them, if something happens. If you purchase Disability Insurance and you become disabled, that insurance could potentially pay your payment for as long as you are disabled or even pay of the entire loan if you are permanently disabled, BUT you have to know about that insurance and notify the company. If you did not know you were paying for that insurance or benefit, you could end up paying your payment for years without even knowing that you had insurance you were paying for that should make those payments. You need to be able to file for this insurance and need the insurance paperwork explaining what you need to do. The same goes with an extended warranty. If something happens to your car, you want to be able to file to get your car fixed or need to be able to know where to send in a copy of the bill if you need to get reimbursed for covered items from the warranty. That is the reason that you need to READ EVERYTHING BEFORE YOU SIGN. The last thing about financing, Make sure to ask if you pay the loan off early, if there is any PRE-PAYMENT PENALTY and ask them to show you on the contract that there is NO PRE-PAYMENT PENALTY. It is rare in this day and age, but it used to be fairly common, that you had to pay the full amount of every payment, including interest, even if you paid the loan off early. In other words, as an example, you would end up paying off interest that you never even owed, if you ended up paying the car off in say two years instead of three. You paid the full interest for the third year even though you paid it off after just two years. AVOID PRE-PAYMENT PENALTIES IF AT ALL POSSIBLE.

BANKS & CREDIT UNIONS

CHECKING ACCOUNTS

In today's day and age it amazes me how so few people have checking accounts. I know that sometimes the reason has to do with not thinking that you have enough excess money but keep this in mind. There are several reasons that you can have a bank account that actually saves you money. It is true that with all the changes enacted recently by Congress, banks are scrambling for new ways to make money since many of the fees that they relied upon previously have been limited by Federal Law but if you spend a little time looking around and calling you can find one that can actually save you money.

Finding an account that does not charge you a monthly fee is the number one thing. Call around or drop in to various local banks, credit unions or financial institutions. Many are personal and friendly folks. Let them know that you are looking for an account that has little or no monthly fees and see what they have to offer.

At various times I have seen offers such as if you open an account they will give you free gifts or even free money. I read in the fine print of one institution that was offering free $100 if you placed a deposit of a certain amount in their bank (I think it was $2,500). There is usually some sort catch, so make sure that you read everything before you sign. I think the one I read that was offering the free $100 for opening an account, the money was placed into your account after a period of time of keeping an active account with them (six months or a year).

DIRECT DEPOSIT

Many Financial Institutions will offer you free checking if you have your paycheck direct deposited into your bank. This could be a wonderful opportunity to save yourself money two ways. 1) You don't have to pay to have your paycheck cashed. I know some large department and food stores offer to have your paychecks cashed but it usually requires a fee be paid to them for the effort. That money is better left in your pocket. 2) You may be able to get the free checking that may allow you various ways to access ALL of your money without any fees withdrawn.

PAYING BILLS ONLINE

Many financial institutions offer free bill paying online. With the cost of postage and gas in today's day and age that can add up to a pretty penny. Why spend money on postage and envelopes to send to your creditors when you can place their information under your bill pay account and with the press of a button your payment is sent so that it is received at the time of your choosing. In addition, if you are driving down to the local water company or electric company every month to pay your bill, with the price of gasoline at between $3.00 and $4.00 per gallon, more power to you, but there may be a less costly and simpler way of getting it there. You can use the money for something else that you need or want.

One additional thing you might want to check out is your financial institutions policy of Non-Sufficient Fund's (NSF) Charges. When you pay a bill online many banks will give you up to closing time to make a deposit to make sure that you do not get hit with a Non-Sufficient Funds charge.

A non-sufficient funds charge is what they used to call a bad check charge. These charges can be very expensive. If you do not pay attention to how much you have in your account and you end up overdrawing the account then you could get a charge from whomever you wrote a check to that overdrew the account PLUS you can get charged by the bank.

ATM FEES

Many banks and credit unions offer free ATM Fees from other banks, particularly if they are a smaller bank with not a bunch of offices in the local area. See what the policy regarding ATM withdrawal and what the charges are if any. Be careful though. When you use an ATM from another bank your bank can charge a fee as well as the other bank may charge a fee so its very important to check this out.

SAVE ON CHECK CASHING & MONEY ORDER FEES

Remember, if you are running your life without a bank account now, you are probably paying fees for every Money Order or even to cash your paycheck. These fees can add up to large amounts of money when added all together over a period of time. If you can find an Bank or Credit Union that you like and that has free checking that you can totally eliminate those fees.

VISA/MASTER CARD ATM CARDS

Most banks and financial institutions will give you access to an ATM card. This ATM card usually doubles as either a Master Card or Visa and allows you to access the money in your account as if it was a Master Card or Visa. This allows you to use it wherever these credit cards are able to be used, restaurants, stores and even online. Most times without any additional charges.

OVERDRAFT FEES – OPT IN OR OUT – YOUR CHOICE

One of the recent changes that was enacted by Congress is that banks or financial institutions have to offer you an option to do one of two things. If a check comes in that you filled out to a creditor, at their option, the bank can pay that check so that the creditor never even knows that you did not have enough money to cover the check and thereby saves you a NSF Fee from the creditor, however the bank will no doubt charge you a NSF or Overdraft fee for the Overdraft Protection. In addition they may charge you a fee daily until you bring the balance current. You can also choose to not have the bank or financial institution pay the check and send it back to the creditor as Non-Sufficient Funds, meaning there was not enough money in the account to cover the check, but this could be equally bad for you with additional fees.

This in a nutshell, is why if you open a bank account, it's VERY IMPORTANT to have a handle on how much you have in your bank account at all times. You can check your balance at an ATM also but make sure that the financial institutions don't charge you for this. The bank fees can eat you alive which is why many are scared of using a bank account. Remember - In most cases if you know what the fees are and how to avoid them, then life will be far less complicated. As with anything else in life .Knowledge is power.

ONE LAST THING – IF IN DOUBT, ASK FOR THE MANAGER!

If you ever have any questions that were not answered by the people you are talking to then ask for their manager. The manager is the person in charge and is much more familiar with what the bank or financial institution can and will do to get and retain your business. ALWAYS ASK FOR THEM when you can get a satisfactory answer from who you are dealing with. That is why managers are there, to get things resolved for their customers, so they stay customers. These are the people and businesses that want your business. See what they can come up with that will help you stay a customer.

Below is an excellent web site that has some very interesting and pertinent information on everything from loans, lending, credit cards, etc.:

http://truthfullending.com

FINANCIAL SERVICES –

WARNING! DO YOUR RESEARCH BEFORE INVESTING.

I am not going to spend a lot of time on this as there are entire library's written about this subject. Suffice it to say that you should always do your research before you invest. Start small and make consistent donations over a long period of time. Let your money work for you. Take advantage of time and interest compounding. Your balances will fluctuate as the stock market does, but in the long run you should be able to do well as long as you don't need to take the money out when a low period hits in the market.

If you are risk averse and one of those people that cannot sleep at night worrying about your money, or if you are closer to retirement that you will start needing to cash some of your portfolio in within ten years or less, you might want to choose safer bets, such as an index fund which has a large and diverse grouping of investments in their portfolios. Many times these funds will not have the steep highs and lows that investing in individual stocks may. If on the other hand you are an individual who has lots of time before you are looking to retire where you could accept some losses if you choose some losing investments you may want to consider individual stocks from companies that you choose. In choosing individual stocks I might suggest that you are the type of individual that truly enjoys the stock market and the researching of individual stock as this type of investing takes a lot more hands on. You should keep an active eye out on what the stock market is doing in general as well as the news on companies that you choose and consider how it might affect your investments.

DIVERSIFY

I know that you have all heard the old saying, "Don't keep all of you eggs in one basket." There is no truer saying than with stocks and investments. The key to a healthy investment strategy is to DIVERSIFY. Research multiple places to put your money into. It doesn't have to be twenty places but a gentle mix of maybe four to eight sound investment choices that are not all inter related. By this I mean, make sure that your investments aren't all in the same grouping like an example would be the "Energy Sector". These would all be investments based on the production, managing and selling of energy products like oil, gas, coal & electricity. You might think that gas and electric have nothing to do with each other but they are all interlinked. While this area can be lucrative at times, especially when gas prices are high, they are also highly susceptible to political turmoil in the oil producing countries and tend to fall off as oil process drop. Make sure even if you are buying something like Index funds that they are not all purchasing stocks from the same groupings. This information would be available in the Prospectus which you can get from your Investment Company or even check online before you invest. A Prospectus is a book or manual dealing with individual stocks or funds telling what they invest in and the information that investors might want to know.

TAX IMPLICATIONS AND CAPITOL GAINS TAX

Whatever type of investing that you choose to be involved in, make sure to check with your tax consultant or Accountant on what Capital Gains Tax is and what the tax ramifications are of the trades that you make. This is one of the first things that you should be familiar with, especially if you are purchasing individual stocks for short term and then re-selling them. It sure would be a major blow to you after buying and selling stocks all year and thinking you made a pretty penny and congratulating yourself only to be hit with a huge tax bill when you file your taxes that year. Believe me, it happens all the time. This goes back to learning from other people's mistakes.

CHOOSING AN INVESTMENT COMPANY: DISCOUNT OR FULL SERVICE?

When you have enough money to invest, there are a lot of options out there. Obviously with all of the frauds and recent misuse of funds that have occurred, it is ALWAYS imperative to research BEFORE you give your hard earned money to someone or a company to invest. This may not be a ton of money in the global economy, but it is all that you have scraped up. You want to do the best with it that you can for yourself and your future.

Keep in mind that your overall goal is to get the best possible investment choices at most affordable rates. In keeping with this goal look around and do your research. If you were the type of person who has an active interest in stocks and the stock market and will be following and investing on your own information and research, you may want to consider what is known as a Discount Broker. This would be a company that has inexpensive trades where you can purchase and sell stocks for as little as $9.99 each trade or possible even less. If you are searching for this type of broker you may want to check the tools that each broker offers, and the trade fees. Also, check and see how easy it is to set up so that you can start placing small amounts of money consistently to this account and any fees that would be associated. Many of these sites offer free real time quotes (what a stock is selling to the minute). You need to make sure and be working with real time quotes if you are going to make split second decisions.

On the other hand, if you are the type of person that wants to make a few wise investments and just let them sit in the account for long periods of time, you may want to consider what is considered a Full Service Broker. These companies have large divisions that keep their eyes and fingers on the pulse on the market and may make suggestions to you on products and services. They usually charge more for this service as you might expect. CAUTION: If you choose this type of broker be VERY CAREFUL to take the investments advice and try to do a little research on your own to verify the information that you are being told BEFORE you invest. Remember it is your money, and it is up to YOU on where you want to invest it. Do not be too complacent. Remember no matter how much you want to believe, there are the Bernie Madoff's of the world out there and many of the people that were taken in that scheme were what was considered savvy investors. This is the rare instance but do not EVER walk blindly into an investment.

When looking for a broker to invest with, the first thing that I suggest is to look at proven winners. What I mean by that is to look for large companies that have been in business for a long time and have a proven track record. There are no guarantees when it comes to investments, but the more risk that you can eliminate the better. As all of the disclaimers say when dealing with any information from investment companies, "past performance data is not a prediction or guarantee of future results" you may at least know that a larger company has been in existence for a long time, many times for decades. They are governed by rules and regulations by the Securities and Exchange Commission (SEC) that oversees the banks and financial institutions. In short, the SEC's job is to protect the investor. For more information on how to invest and where to start your research, please check with the SEC website listed below:

http://investor.gov/

Below is a great link from the SEC on 12 Savings and Investing Tips from 2012:

http://investor.gov/news-alerts/investor-bulletins/12-saving-investing-tips-2012

401K

Many people start investing from their workplaces with a 401K. This is a terrific way to start, as they many times are taken out of your paychecks as pre-tax dollars. What this means is, they take the money out for your 401K before you pay taxes on that portion. (Example – Your paycheck would normally be $1000 and you put $100 into your 401K. You would actually pay taxes on $900 instead of the $1000.) This can actually save you additional money in taxes because many times you end up paying a lower amount of taxes because it is based on the figure AFTER your 401K deductions have happened.

In addition, if your company offers a matching contribution of up to a certain amount of what you put in yourself, this turns out to be extra money for you to build upon. This in my book, is like having FREE money. If you were to contribute $100 and your company's policy is to match 15%, then the company would contribute an additional $15 for every hundred dollars that you invested in your 401K. Sometimes companies will say that you have to work for them say 5 years (depends on the company) to be fully vested in the potion that they contribute. This would only affect the amount they contributed, not anything you have contributed. It means that you would be vested, or ELIGIBLE to keep 100% of what they matched after a five year period of time. It may be something like 20% per year up to the full amount after five years or something. Check and see if your company offers a 401K matching program. The more that you can afford to put away at an earlier age, the better it should be for your long term growth of the retirement savings.

There is one more thing to keep in mind, because 401K's are PRE-TAX Dollars, you have not paid taxes on them yet. Keep this in mind and check with your tax consultant or preparer if you end up leaving a job and want to CASH the money in. It means there could be taxes and penalties that you have to pay for early withdrawal of funds.

COMPANY STOCK OPTIONS

While working for many companies in today's society, you may have the opportunity to invest in the company that you work for. Some people advise against this. This choice is up to you. Even on the SEC website link listed above they suggest not to invest too heavily into your employers stock. If you believe in your company and they are offering what you consider a fair deal on purchasing the company stock, than you may want to invest SOME of your hard earned money. I would certainly say if you invest in your own company, you should have only a small portion of your full investment portfolio. Many of the people that were working for WorldCom or Enron invested their life savings only to wind up with nothing or at the very least pennies on every dollar invested after those companies came crashing down.

The last thing I will say about investing in company stock. Keep in mind that there are laws that govern the selling of insider stock if you are a person who is in a position to know insider information that the normal public would not have access to that same information. In addition you should be aware again on the purchase and selling of company stock and how Capital Gains Tax will be affected when you file your taxes. I would suggest checking with your tax consultant or Accountant.

CREDIT CARDS

HOW TO GET THE MOST FOR YOUR MONEY

The world of credit cards is ever evolving. With the Credit Card act of 2009, the rules have been changed to reduce the fees that credit card companies can charge and unfair rate increases as well as plain sight language disclosure which makes it a little easier than it used to be to get through the legal mumbo-jumbo that have always been a part of any credit card companies fine print. While it does not alleviate your responsibility to read and understand what you are signing, it should make the language a bit clearer to understand.

The link to the Credit Card Act and the changes it represents is below:

http://www.whitehouse.gov/the_press_office/Fact-Sheet-Reforms-to-Protect-American-Credit-Card-Holders

ANNUAL FEES

Keep in the back of your mind that what you ultimately want from a credit card is a line of credit with a company that reports your payment history to the Credit Bureaus and has the lowest amount of interest rate and fees possible. I know this is a lot to consider and compare, but it isin keeping with your goal of reducing your overall monthly bills and debts. As part of researching a possible credit card you are considering applying for, you should always ask if there is an Annual Fee. If there is an Annual Fee, shop around and see if try to find another card that does not have an annual fee. Is there something that this card offers that is essential to you that other cards do not? If not, move on to another company. Remember every time you apply for a loan or any form of credit it will affect your credit rating, so check into the credit cards BEFORE you apply for one. If a creditor sees you applying to several banks, this might indicate that you are having financial problems that are forcing you to use your credit cards for a lot of daily expenditures. In addition, if they see you applying to multiple places it leaves them with an unknown factor. They have to consider when extending you credit if you can afford to pay the loan or credit card back. The unknown factor is, a Credit Bureau may show that you applied for credit. It does not show if they extended you the credit. It takes time to get credit limits and amounts owed onto your credit report. It may take several months to cycle through. What this means to the creditor is that they have to assume if you have shown yourself credit worthy (have the ability and the intent to repay the credit requested) then you would probably have been credit worthy to the other lender also. This means they have to figure that you were granted the credit lines requested at each of the places you applied. If this is the case, it could throw your Debt to Payment ratio way out of line and ultimately decide that if you had all of these lines of credit that you could not afford all of these payments. They may decide to pass on the loan or line of credit. Banks and financial institutions do not like unknowns when granting credit.

INTEREST

It goes without saying that when looking for a credit line or credit card, you want to look for the lowest interest rate possible. Remember, the ultimate goal is to use the card only in emergencies and/or to pay off monthly so that you do not have to pay any interest charges. Think of how you use your credit. Do you carry a balance? Do you pay for things that you get Money Back or Frequent Flyer Miles or Points and pay off monthly? If you do have a credit card balance that you carry, you want to get any balance to the credit card that you have that has the lowest annual percentage rate and preferably, no annual fee.

PAYOFF & CASH CHECK OFFERS – CASH COSTS MORE!

VERY IMPORTANT – Banks and Financial Institutions that handle your credit card account, most times, will charge you a MUCH HIGHER interest rate for CASH ADVANCES or CHECKS CASHED that they sent to you then they would charge for Goods and Services that you purchased. If you need to place something on a credit card, call who you want to pay off first or visit them in person and ask if they take Master Card, Visa, American Express, Discover, etc. If they do accept the credit card that you have, use your credit card to pay the bill directly. This way if you have chosen your credit card company wisely, they should charge the lower interest rate charge for goods and services. If you end up using a check that the Credit Card Company sent to you to put cash in your account, you will be probably be charged the much higher interest rate for Cash Advances plus there may be additional check cashing fees that would be applied also. READ AND KEEP all information that is sent to you with any checks from your credit card company. If you use the checks, keep the information that came with them so you can make sure they follow through with their promise. Make a copy of the check used for your records if you can.

If you have ever had a credit card, you have probably received a page of checks in one form or another. Sometimes they are a part of your monthly statement. Sometimes you will receive a letter from your credit card holder with a page of checks and a letter saying something to the effect of NEED EXTRA CASH or PAY OFF OTHER CREDITORS. As always, read everything extremely carefully before you use any of these checks. Sometimes, if you pay off other higher interest credit cards and the fees and interest rates are low enough it may make sense to use them. One additional thing to keep in mind with these checks used, when you normally put goods or servies on your credit card there is a Grace Period which usually is around 25 days or one billing cycle where no interest is charged if you pay off monthly. This allows you to purchase something and wait to pay for it when you get the bill without having to pay interest on your purchase. When you use one of the checks that are sent to you, read the information carefully. If you are getting a Cash Advance, then you will be probably be charged from the date of the transaction (the day you cash the check). This means you are paying the interest rate immediately. These are things to consider when you are trying io decide if you truly NEED that money or just WANT the money.

WORD OF WARNING – Remember what I said earlier in this book, when you have to get rid of things like Bank Checks that have been sent to you through the mail or credit card offers that say preapproved and old bank statements or stuff that has your personal information on them. ALWAYS DESTROY THESE PAPERS. Burn them, shred them and place in separate garbage bags, never the same one. Put the shredded paper in the garden to make mulch. Cover your credit and destroy these things so others can't benefit from you hard work.

PAY OFF YOUR HIGHEST INTEREST CREDIT CARD 1ST

Try to avoid having monthly credit card debt if possible. If you do happen to have multiple credit cards, take your highest interest credit card and pay that one down as quickly as you can. Then take the next highest credit card and do the same. Always try to make as much as you can in a payment. If you just pay off the minimum payments each time, it could literally take years to pay them down, even if you do not take any more advances or buy anything else. Once you pay off a credit card, try and stick it somewhere safe, like in a safe deposit box at your bank. This way it would be accessible if you ever needed it in case of an emergency but you would be far less likely to use the card to get yourself into trouble or spend frivolously on something you don't need.

If you have multiple credit cards, try to combine them if possible. Call your lowest interest credit card and let them know that you would be interested in using their card in paying off other creditors. See what they would be willing to do to help you. They might be able to offer to pay them off with no fees just to gain the business if you have been a valued customer.

POINTS, CASH BACK AND FREQUENT FLYER MILES

When you look into a Credit Card, many lenders offer such things as Rewards Cards. These cards may offer things such as Frequent Flyer Miles on a certain airline, a percentage Cash Back, Points to be used for future stays at a hotel or some other offer. Keep in mind, the best thing for your budget is NOT TO USE CREDIT CARDS. Look at these promotions extremely carefully so that you know all of the details. Ask yourself:

- Do the Frequent Flyer Miles Expire?

- Is there an Annual Fee?

- What are the charges involved?

- What are the rules?

- Does the card have a high Annual Percentage Rate if you carry a balance?

Remember the adage: You won't find something for nothing. Usually you will find that there is some sort of gimmick. If the institution is giving something away, then they are making it back up in some other way. I would only suggest using these or any credit cards if you are a person who can track what your spending in your head, and can pay off the balance every month. If you only buy what you would normally buy anyway such as food, gas, normal expenses, then it may make sense if you can get something back, but you truly need to be careful what you choose.

IF YOU HAVE THEM, KNOW WHAT THEY CAN DO FOR YOU!

For those of you that do have credit cards, you should know the secondary benefits they offer. When you sign up to get a credit card, once you are approved they will send you a welcome packet that tells you what specific discounts or advantages their credit card include for you. Some of those specific benefits, other than points might be useful if you ever need them. If you don't read them and know which card offers which benefit, you may lose out. Some of the great benefits of various credit cards that I have seen are:

• REPLACEMENT COVERAGE – If you purchase an item with this card, and it is broken or destroyed within a certain amount of time, they will pay to replace that item.

• FREE TRAVEL INSURANCE – If you use their card to purchase your airline tickets it also includes free travelers insurance if you happen to lose your life in an airline accident.

• FREE RENTAL CAR UPGRADE – By using their credit card at a certain Rental Car Company you can get the next sized car upgrade at no additional charge.

• CAR RENTAL INSURANCE – Many credit cards will offer the optional Car Rental Insurances that can break the bank. Check and see if your does.

• LOST LUGGAGE PROTECTION – Certain cards can offer you a daily amount if your luggage is ever lost until it is found (there are maximum amounts).

• FREE IDENTITY THEFT PROTECTION – If you are ever the victim of Identity Theft, they will pay a certain amount of fees and services toward getting you back to life as normal.

• PRESALE TICKETS AND PREEFERRED SEATING – For concerts & events.

• DISCOUNT ATTRACTIONS – Many of the credit cards offer discounts on certain amusement parks and attractions. As an example, Bank of America has a program called "Museums On Us" for their card members that have 150 museums that you can get into with free admission on certain days. For more info visit: **http://museums.bankofamerica.com/**

• ROADSIDE ASSISTANCE – Check and see what your credit cards policy is. Some credit cards offer some bare-bones roadside assistance to get you to a local garage if you don't have a Roadside Assistance Plan that you are already paying for.

Obviously from the examples listed above it is vital to know what your credit cards offer or you could be missing out on a considerable amount of valuable perks. I mean if you are going to have them and use them then at least know which one to use.

DON'T BE TAKEN ADVANTAGE OF – FIGHT BACK!

If you feel that you have been taken advantage of by an unscrupulous or fraudulent company, you can fight back many times if you used your credit card to purchase the goods or services. Money Crashers put together an excellent article on how to handle disputes with vendors and businesses and the steps to follow if you ever need to resolve a dispute with a company that you had dealings with. You can see the article here.

http://www.moneycrashers.com/credit-card-chargebacks-process-rules/

PRE-PAID CREDIT CARDS

I always encourage people avoid these cards if possible. There are some that are better than others. Some have an excessive amount of fees. As with any other suggestion in this book, investigate and find who has the lowest fees if you decide you just can't live without them. Remember, many of these companies are just letting you use your own money for a fee, just so you can use a Master Card or Visa. You could do the same thing by putting your money in a bank account and getting an ATM card for nothing. There is no risk to them and many high fees are usually charged.

If you are interested in reading what five top prepaid cards that About.com recommends, please follow the link below:

http://credit.about.com/od/prepaidcardreviews/tp/Best-Prepaid-Cards.htm

REAL ESTATE

SELLERS HAVE A DECISION TO MAKE – TO SELL OR NOT TO SELL?

I know we have taken an enormous loss in the Real Estate Market in the last few years. This has changed many minds. I also know that many homeowners are what is called, "under water or upside down" in their homes, when it comes to their mortgages. This means that many people find themselves in the unfortunate situation where they owe more for their mortgage than their home is worth. As with anything, there is an upper level that someone will pay for a product or service. This is called a market ceiling. With homes, many neighborhoods are hindered with large amounts of foreclosures and it has only gotten worse when unemployment is rampant. If someone is unemployed, then they probably don't have any income coming in. If they have no income, it begs to reason they can't pay their bills, including their mortgage, which leaves them susceptible to foreclosure. When a neighborhood gets many foreclosures, it lowers the values of the homes around them. The reason for this is, the homeowner is trying to sell their home, at a time when there are large amounts of foreclosures in their area. They may find themselves competing in the price range set by the foreclosure homes in their area. The banks and financial institutions are trying to sell these foreclosures just to get them off of their books and get the money back into something that is MAKING them money, not losing their money.

When a Real Estate agent pulls "Comps" or "Comparable Home Sales" from the last six months to a year for potential buyers (also sellers looking to list their home for sale), they look at three things:

1.) Listing Price – of homes of comparable size and amenities to yours in your same area.

2.) Selling Price – of homes of comparable size and amenities as yours in the same area.

3.) Time on the Market – How long those houses that did sell were actively being sold before the deal went through.

Buyers always look to get the best price and best "value added" benefits they can for their money. These value added benefits can be anything from offering to help the potential buyer with their closing costs to lowering the amount of money that the buyer has to come up with as a down payment. Other incentives that can help sweeten the deal for a potential buyer are negotiating to let the buyer keep appliances, window treatments or even a particular piece of furniture that the buyer likes in a room. These are all things that usually cost the seller money.

Each seller has to decide what they can afford to offer the buyer, as an incentive to purchase their home. The buyer may be comparing yours to other homes down the street or in the same area. With a large amount of foreclosures in an area, it makes it harder for the actual owner/occupied sellers because many times they do not have the deep pockets that a bank has and the recent comps show much lower home sale prices due to the sale of foreclosed properties or homes still on the market that your competing against.

BUYERS - GET A GOOD DEAL – BUY RIGHT!

Real Estate has classically been one of the best investments for the average person on the street. Well guess what. It still is. I know that there have been numerous issues facing the real Estate Market in the last several years what with the Mortgage debacle, Foreclosure mess, Robo-signing and the Real Estate Market taking an enormous loss in many areas of the country.

If you are in Real Estate Market as a buyer, there is only one secret. That key is like anything else that you buy, BUY AT THE RIGHT PRICE. If you are searching for a home right now, if you have handled your credit rating wisely and are lucky enough to have a decent job then you can take advantage of some of the best Interest Rates EVER and you can also get some homes at the best prices in years. Keep in mind, no one actually knows where the bottom of the Real Estate Market is, but there has been such a substantial shift from the market Highs, that you should start looking for the best deal possible.

I have a few web sites listed below where you can start your research. These are actual Government Web Sites that have HUD and other Government Foreclosed Homes listed. Some places are charging many times the cost of this book for just the access to the information in these two web sites listed below. Good Luck, God Bless and HAPPY HOME HUNTING.

GOVERNMENT OWNED PROPERTY & FORECLOSURE WEBSITES – YOU COULD GET SOME AWESOME DEALS!!!

http://homesales.gov/homesales/mainAction.do

http://bidselect.com

FREDDIE MAC OWNED HOMES

http://www.homesteps.com/featuresearch.html

MORTGAGES

WHAT IS IN A MORTGAGE PAYMENT?

When you purchase what is considered Real Property (Real Estate) unless you pay for the property cash which for most of us is not possible you will end up paying a mortgage payment. The sale included two things the Deed which grants ownership to the person listed on the Deed. Then there is the Mortgage or "Note" which is the promise to repay the loan (agreed upon amount) to pay off the home and get the Deed. This is usually done by paying a Mortgage Payment. The Mortgage Payment, if it is from a bank or financial institution, will usually include four things.

1.) Principal – The amount you are paying off of the purchase price of the property.

2.) Interest – The amount of interest you are paying to borrow money.

3.) Taxes – The amount of state, county and local taxes owed yearly on your home.

4.) Insurance – The amount that is paid out to cover the home with Homeowners
Insurance and Flood Insurance (if required) and Private Mortgage Insurance (if required).

Combined these will equal the actual Mortgage Payment that you will end up paying.

INTEREST ONLY – ARE THERE ANY BENEFITS?

Interest Only Mortgages are one type of loan to be wary of. This type of loan, is primarily for people who receive their income spaced over long periods of time such as derived from infrequent commissions, bonuses or royalties. This would not be something that you would want necessarily, if you had a regular income. These loans are generally set for a fixed term, typically five to ten years. Your payments, which are interest only (no principal), so the loan amount at the end of the term would still be the same as when you began your payments, unless you aid additional toward principal.

At the end of that term, you would either pay off the loan in full, refinance or start paying off the principal. Obviously, if you chose to begin to pay off the principal this would be a much larger payment than you were accustomed to paying, with the principal added in.

If you are expecting an inheritance in say five years, this may be an acceptable option to consider. If you are expecting a large increase in income at a later date, then you might also consider this loan. If you need a smaller payment and want the flexibility to pay as much toward the principal as you can, then it might be an option.

I am normally against ANYTHING that ties up future income or is based on future EXPECTATIONS. We never know what the future holds. I don't like leaving things up to chance. Do your research and if you decide its right for you, check and make sure there are no Pre-payment Penalties and that you can pay off Principal amounts, at any time, without penalty if you so decide. It will, however, give you a significantly lower payment in the short term, especially in the introductory period.

ADJUSTABLE RATE MORTAGES

Adjustable Rate Mortgages (ARM) are usually set up and maintain an initial interest rate for a set period of time (standard is one, three or five year periods). Your interest rate will change at the end of that term, either up or down, depending on what has happened with the Index that your payment is tied to. Be aware, many times the initial period has an INTRODUCTORY or promotional rate much lower than you would normally pay.

ARM products are tied to an index which may be something like one, three or five year Treasury Securities. It can also be tied to other rates such as the Prime Rate (the lowest amount of money that a financial institution may borrow from another lender). These rates may be set up in your mortgage something to the effect of Prime Rate plus 5.99% (Margin). What this means is, if Prime Rate on the day that your loan is closed is 3.25% and your rate was Prime + 5.99% than the actual rate that you would be paying is 9.24% until the next adjustment. Keep in mind these are just examples. The Margin can vary due to the lender's own guidelines and your own individual credit worthiness.

There is something usually included in an Adjustable Rate Mortgage that is called a CAP. This means that the lender is Capped from increasing their rate more than a certain amount at any given time, when they come due, by whatever is agreed upon. The reason for this is to make sure that the loan does not become an undue hardship for the customer in times of highly volatile interest rate changes.

A couple of other things to be aware of with ARM's, they may have Prepayment Penalties if you pay the loan off early, where you may have to pay certain fees. The other thing to be wary of with these loans is that they can have a Negative amortization. This means, if the amount of your mortgage payment is not enough to cover the interest portion on the loan for that period, the excess interest is added back into your loan so that you actually OWE MORE FOR YOUR LOAN than you originally took out. You could end up paying interest on the interest.

For more info on Adjustable Rate Mortgages, you can go to Wikipedia to help you get more information, among other places:

http://en.wikipedia.org/wiki/Adjustable-rate_mortgage

FIXED RATE MORTGAGE – 15 OR 30 YEAR TERM?

Most people who buy a home end up getting a Fixed Rate Mortgage for a term of either 15 or 30 years. Obviously your payment will be higher on a 15 year loan, but you will be paying thousands of dollars less in interest charges. Much more of your payment goes toward the Principal (the amount that you own of the home). This is a marvellous thing if you can afford the slightly higher payment.

Most times the rate of interest charged by the lender is less on the 15 year term. That extra 15 years could end up costing you tens or even hundreds of thousands more in interest charges.

You can go to the below link to calculate the difference in saving between a 15 year and 30 year mortgage. Remember this will only give you the Principal and Interest portions of your payment.

http://www.bankrate.com/calculators/mortgages/15-year-30-year-mortgage-calculator.aspx?ec_id=m1023581&ef_id=amFPZyJR2wIAAI3V:201207 12125309:s

THREE DAY RECISION

The Three Day Recision period is only available on certain Home Equity Loans and Refinances. Under the Truth In Lending Act, which was enacted to shield borrowers from predatory or unscrupulous lenders, you may get what is called a Three Day Recision Period. This is a cooling off period for you to be able to look at all the paperwork and decide if you want to go through with the loan or not. If you do not want to go through with the loan, you contact your lender within three days and notify them IN WRITING that you want to Rescind or Cancel the loan. Let the lender know that you have changed your mind, BEFORE you borrow the money, and by law the lender is responsible to relinquish any rights to any claim to your collateral and refund any fees you have paid. When it comes to loans, don't get bullied either by a lender or someone who may be asking you for money from the proceeds of the loan. REMEMBER – You are the one taking out the loan AND responsible for paying it back. This is particularly important when a loan is tied to your home. You could literally lose your house if the payments are not made per the agreement. Do not rely on someone else. DO NOT TAKE LOANS OUT FOR OTHER PEOPLE. YOU COULD GET BURNED. BADLY!

PRIVATE MORTGAGE INSURANCE – WHAT IS IT?

Private Mortgage Insurance (PMI) is one of the most expensive insurances out there on the market, and it may be required by lenders if you are putting down less than 20%.on a home that you will be living in (owner occupied). Let's say that you are buying a home valued at $100,000, and you are putting down 10% ($10,000). In this instance, you are at 90% Loan to Value (LTV) or 90% of your home is mortgaged to the lender and 10% t is what you are putting down or your Equity. The PMI only covers the 80% and above, so if you were required to pay PMI than the amount that you are paying monthly to the PMI portion of your loan is Insurance for just $10,000. PMI is insurance that you, the borrower, are paying as part of your mortgage payment that covers the lender in the event that you default on the loan. Remember lenders may require a higher Loan to Value ratio on Rental Properties before they agree to remove the PMI.

KNOW YOUR RIGHTS – Look into the Homeowners Protection Act of 1998 - If your loan was closed on July 29, 1999 or later and was for $252,700 (as of Jan. 1, 2000) it should be considered a "Conforming Loan" to the guidelines enacted under the law. In addition, if your loan was not considered a "high risk" loan, than your lender should be required to notify you when you pay your principal amount down to 80% of the original sale price. If they notify you of this, it is your responsibility to contact them and ask them to remove the PMI portion of your payment. I believe, if you take no action, they are required to remove the PMI automatically at 78% but please check with your lender and research on your own or you could be paying hundreds, if not thousands of dollars in extra PMI premiums for insurance that is not needed or required by law.

You should keep a close eye on the value of your home yourself and ask to have the PMI removed as soon as possible to save the most amount of money possible. Ask a Realtor to do a Competitive Market Analysis of your home to see what comparable homes are selling for in your area. If your area has bucked the downward spiraling in real estate prices or as future real estate prices begin to escalate again you may have the opportunity to have the PMI removed.

If you feel that your home has increased in value a great deal since purchasing the home, check with your lender and ask them if you pay for an appraisal, and it shows you are now at 80% LTV (Loan Amount to Value of home) or lower, will they take the PMI off of your mortgage? If you are a valued customer and have paid well on the loan, they will probably say they would agree to do this. Make notes with whom you spoke to and get this in writing. MAKE SURE TO ASK FOR A LIST OF APPROVED REAL ESTATE APPRAISERS THAT THEY WOULD ACCEPT. The last thing that you would want to do is pay for $300 to $400 for an appraisal that the lender will not accept. This is a little known tact to save you potentially thousands of dollars.

REFINANCING – DOES IT MAKE SENSE?

The key with refinancing is to look at the cost of refinancing your mortgage and what your ultimate savings are going to be. Keep in mind that there are fees involved in refinancing your home. Make sure to get an itemized list of what those closing costs will be. The easiest way to find out if it makes sense to refinance is to consider how long you plan on being in your home and add up the total amount of closing costs.

EXAMPLE:

Let's say that the total closing costs will be $3,500, and you will be financing for 15 years (180 months). Your payment will go down $100 per month. In this instance, you would divide your total closing costs by the monthly savings in your payments.

$3,500 divided by $100 monthly savings = 35 months. So the breakeven point on your loan would be 35 months. After that, each month you would save $100 for the remainder of your loan. 180 months – 35 months = 145 months X $100 = $14,500 in savings over the loan period (after breaking even at 35 months). Just make sure you have the accurate costs and what your monthly savings will be and use the formula above.

Now I mentioned earlier, if you plan on moving in three years or less, it would not make sense to refinance in this instance above because you would not break even for 35 months.

SOME OF THE COSTS ASSOCIATED WITH REFINANCING.

Lending Fees – Flat fees charged by the lender to process a mortgage.

Appraisal Fee – A fee charged by the Appraisal Company to appraise the value of your home (typically $300 to $400)

Points – These include such fees as Discount Fees (the amount a lender will allow you to pay up front to reduce the interest rate you will pay) and Origination Fees (a fee used to reimburse the originator of the loan - 1 point equals 1% of the mortgage amount) – The lender will many times allow you to add these fees into the loan.

Credit Fees – These are the fee charged to run your credit history.

Insurance Fees – A current Homeowners Insurance Policy (plus Flood Insurance will also normally be required by the lender if your home is in a flood prone area). The lender will require replacement cost coverage. You probably already had these insurances on your home with your current lender if you are refinancing.

Escrow and Title Fees – Title Insurance will insure both lender and owner of having clear title to the property. This way, someone doesn't come in later down the line and say they are the true owners.
Escrow Fees are service fees charged by the title company.

Taxes – The lender will require that there are no delinquent property taxes on the home that could encumber the mortgaged property with a valid lien.

RECASTING – A POSSIBLE OPTION IF YOU CANT REFINANCE.

Recasting is a relatively new option for some homeowners with fixed rate mortgages. Recasting is when a homeowner wants to put down a substantial amount on the unpaid principal owed on their home and have the loan re-amortized based on the remaining balance of the principal. The loan term and interest rate would still be the same, but the loan payments would be less if they were based on the lower principal amount.

One critical key with Recasting is that the amount you are putting down would be "substantial". This means $5,000 to $10,000 or more. You would have to have to accumulate this money and be able to put it towards your principal amount. It could be a tremendously inexpensive way of saving money in closing costs, which are few, since you are not refinancing the loan. This should also save you additional money on the reduced interest you will pay over the term of the loan. Ask your lender if they would allow you to Recast if it will benefit you and you have the extra money available.

BELOW IS A WEB SITE THAT HAS VARIOUS LOAN CALCULATORS TO HELP YOU DECIDE HOW MUCH OF A HOME YOU CAN AFFORD.

The Amortization Schedule is the most common loan calculator. It will tell you what your payment will be based on the amount of interest you will pay and the term (length of time you have the mortgage). Now keep in mind, the payment calculated will not include your taxes and insurance part of your payment.

http://truthfullending.com/mortgage-financial-calculators/amort-table-calc/

Below is a link that may help you in your research. It has some interesting information and articles on everything from Mortgage Finance to Foreclosure and most things in between.

http://truthfullending.com/

INSURANCES

TRY TO COMBINE POLICIES IF POSSIBLE

One key thing to remember with insurance companies is that like any other consumer oriented company, THEY WANT GOOD CUSTOMERS. You want to pay your bills on time and be a valued customer so these companies WANT YOUR BUSINESS. If you have a home and are ready to purchase a rental property, ask your insurance agent if he can combine your policies to give you a discount on both. If you have your homeowners insurance and your automobile insurance through two different companies, call both companies and see who can offer you the best deal possible if you were to switch to their company for both. Packaging can save you a great deal of money. If you don't ask, then you will never know (or save money).

One additional thing to ask your insurance agent, What discounts you might be able to qualify for? With car insurance, it might be a Safe Driver Discount, certain safety features on your car or having an Anti-Theft Device installed. For homeowners insurance, it can be something as uncomplicated as dead bolt locks on the home or an Alarm System installed. These and many other things can give you discounted rates.

LIFE INSURANCE – TRY TO COVER YOUR LOVED ONES.

One of the most valuable things that you can do for your family is to get some form of life insurance to help them through their time of need when you die. I know, if you are young and single this is the last thing you thinking about. Still consider it, even if it is only enough to get your funeral expenses covered. When you are young and in excellent health not only is it inexpensive to purchase life insurance but many times you are guaranteed, if you make your payments on time, not to be dropped by your insurance carrier, should you ever become uninsurable (get sick to where you would not normally be able to qualify to purchase Life Insurance).

We never want to think of ourselves dying, but the reality is, we all will someday. That being said, it is hard to think about and harder to make pre-arrangements. It is something to keep in mind so that your family does not have to deal with these things at THEIR time of need, when you pass from this world. These are the people that love you the most and will be hurting even without trying to run the gauntlet of the unknown. If you can't deal with this subject now, then you will leave them to deal with it at the time when they may not be thinking clearly. Your loved ones could end up paying for these decisions for years to come.

If you buy Life Insurance when you are young and in robust health, you can get the insurance very inexpensively. You can make your payments in various ways: monthly, quarterly, biyearly (twice per year) or yearly. Keep in mind, you may be able to get life insurance at a good rate through where you work. Check and see with your Personnel Dept. or Human Resources if they offer Life Insurance and see if it's right for you. If they offer it, you can probably have the premiums (payments) taken out of your paycheck so you never have to deal with it. Ask this question of yourself. What would happen to my family if I passed away? If you are married, are you the primary or only income? If so, your family will have an enormous adjustment even without the financial hardship that your death would bring.

Your spouse will have to find work right away. Will there be money for emergency things that come up? Will your family be able to pay the monthly bills? Do you have a mortgage payment? Will they have the money to pay off the home or make the payments? Do you have a substantial amount put away in savings? If the answer to any of these questions alarms you, then you have the ability to put your mind at ease. Look into life insurance for your family.

There are different types of Life Insurance from different providers. The two most common types are Term Life Insurance and Whole Life Insurance.

TERM LIFE INSURANCE – Is usually the least costly form of life insurance. This is a policy where you pay your payments (premiums) for a set period of time If you die during the term of the policy, as long as your premiums are paid up to date, the policy amount would be paid to your beneficiary (the person you choose to get the money in the event you die). You can generally renew your policy and continue the insurance as long as you do not let it lapse (stop paying). You are simply paying for the insurance. With term insurance, your premiums raises in increments as you age. You might pay X amount from age 40 to 49 years old and then 50 to 55 you would pay Y, etc.

WHOLE LIFE INSURANCE - is a whole different animal. Actuaries (Accountants that crunch numbers and statistics) who worked for the insurance companies came up with a policy that had level payments for your entire lifetime. Obviously when you are young your premium would be higher than it would cost to purchase term insurance, so the excess premium money that is spread out over so many years, is placed into a cash account, where the cash and interest will build towards the future payout (death benefit). As you get older, your payments would normally get higher as you aged with Term Insurance but in this type of policy it would be the same from start to finish. It is set to run throughout your whole life.

Here is a fantastic article from Kiplinger Magazine that gives some sound advice on things to consider when it comes to Life Insurance.

http://www.kiplinger.com/magazine/archives/how-much-life-insurance-do-you-need.html

HEALTH INSURANCE

Health Insurance is another extremely valuable type of Insurance to consider for yourself and your family. Did you know that at the time of the writing of this book (July 2012) Medical Expenses are the leading cause for the Filing of Bankruptcies in the United States? It has been for some time. Having good and affordable health insurance is one of the most fundamental ways of having a fit financial life as well as remaining healthy. You only have one body, make sure you keep it as healthy as possible so that it can help you meet all of your other objectives.

In today's day and age of spiraling health care costs one trip to the hospital can cost thousands of dollars, even tens of thousands of dollars. We never think life will happen to us. Well guess what. It does happen to us and others just like us, all the time. You can't hide your head in the sand. Shop around and see what the best alternatives are for yourself and your family. Check into premiums (the payments you pay), costs and what those payments cover. Also check into what the maximum lifetime limits are and while you are checking, find out what the deductible amounts are. A deductible is the amounts that you pay before the insurance kicks in to pay their share.

This is another benefit that many companies offer to their employees, Check with your Personnel Department or Human Resources Department. To find if they offer Health Insurance Options. If your company does offer a Group Health Plan for their employees, this usually helps offset your costs. The company may pay a portion of the cost of the plan. This reduces your insurance cost. It costs less for insurance coverage with your company, as a group policy, than if you were to look for insurance on your own.

Keep in mind, with many work related Health Insurance Plans they offer a time window that you have to join. It may be after three months of employment or at the end of their fiscal year when they have Open Enrollment and take advantage of it. Make sure that you find out if there is a time window that needs to be met. This is an excellent opportunity for those that may have some pre-existing conditions to be able to purchase health coverage when they would not normally qualify for because of their ongoing health issues.

Other helpful resource links are below:

DO YOU QUALIFY FOR MEDICARE – Official Site Below:

http://www.medicare.gov/default.aspx

MEDICAID INFORMATION – State Info – Click on the map and choose your State.

http://www.medicare.gov/default.aspx

DISCOUNTED PRESCRIPTION DRUGS –

THE $4.00 LIST – Go to your local Walmart Pharmacy and ask them for a copy of what is called the $4.00 Prescription List. This is a four or five page list of low cost and Generic Drugs that are available at their pharmacy. Look through the list and see if any of them can replace what you are currently taking and ask your Doctor if they would be right for your budget and your health. I would believe that other Retail Pharmacies have a comparable list, please feel free to check with them.

PARTNERSHIP FOR PRESCRIPTION ASSISTANCE - The site listed below is called the Partnership for Prescription Assistance. It is a large group of Prescription Drug Manufacturers that make their medications available for free or at reduced cost to those that qualify.

https://www.pparx.org/Intro.php

AUTOMOBILE INSURANCE

Automobile Insurance is not only important, it's the law. Check with your state and see what the minimum requirements are. Use these minimums as just that, the bottom base line. They are the minimum required by law. As you accumulate wealth, or increase your income level, you need to keep in mind that you want to cover yourself from losing what you have accumulated over the year from the potential of a lawsuit against you in the event of an automobile accident. Automobile accidents can happen to anyone. They happen every single day. Be prepared with the right type of insurance that meets your needs and with the right deductible amounts. A deductible is the amount that you pay first, before the insurance company kicks in their part, from any claim. If you had an accident and you had a $500 deductible and there was $2500 in covered damages that you would pay the first $500, the insurance company would be responsible for the other $2000 above that.

NOTE: Each of these sections below has a maximum amount that your insurance company will be responsible for. These limits are listed in your policy. Make sure that you cover yourself with limits that are high enough because if someone is injured in an auto accident, they may sue you for any outstanding amount that is not covered by your insurance company.

The basic types of automobile insurance are:

UNINSURED MOTORISTS – Depending on the state, this coverage can cover either damages to property or medical expenses for injury from a driver who does not have liability insurance.

UNDERINSURED MOTORISTS - Depending on the state, this coverage can cover medical expenses for injury from a driver who does not have sufficient liability insurance.

LIABILITY – the cost of damage that you are liable for as a result of an accident. It could be another vehicle, a house you hit or bodily injury to someone in the other car.

MEDICAL PAYMENTS OR PIP (Personal Injury Protection) - This is medical coverage for you and your passengers should injury occur while in your vehicle. Some states require that this coverage pay regardless of who is at fault in the accident. You will sometimes see this on your policy as an amount such as $25,000/$50,000. This means $25,000 per person and up to $50,000 per occurrence.

COLLISION – helps pay for damage or loss sustained to a covered vehicle due to a collision with another car, object or rollover.

COMPREHENSIVE – helps pay for damage or loss sustained to a covered vehicle for other reasons such as Fire, Flood, Hail, Theft, Vandalism, Wind, etc.

HOMEOWNERS INSURANCE

Homeowners insurance is one of the most important forms of insurance you can have as a homeowner. If you have a mortgage, homeowners insurance is probably required by your lender to cover the home they hold the mortgage on as collateral. This way, if something happens to that home, the lender will not take a loss. Make sure to review your coverage's every year at renewal time to make sure that you have enough coverage to meet your needs. Have you had any additions or changes happen to your property within the last year that makes it necessary to increase or change your coverage? Some of these things could be, a home addition or substantial renovation, remodeling, etc. Homeowners Insurance covers six basic types of insurance under a standard policy.

A. Dwelling Coverage – Covers the structural components of your home against damage and possible loss due to covered claims such as fire, hail, hurricane & lightening. Other separate policies may be needed for flood and earthquake insurance.

B. Other Structures on Your Property. – The same coverage as above except for detached garages, sheds and outbuildings, etc. located on your property. Make sure that the amount is adequate to cover these structures in the event of a loss. Many times, an insurer's standard policy, will assess 10% of the replacement value of your home as the amount for other structures, this may not be enough if you have large or valuable structures on your property.

C. Personal Property/Contents – Your personal items and belongings if they are lost due to a covered event. Note – This is not normally replacement value but is normally prorated based on when you purchased the items. Make sure if you have large amounts of jewelry, guns, antiques, artwork and collections to have additional coverage (a rider), which provides extra protection on the items above and beyond the standard limited amounts on this type of items.

D. Loss of Use – provides for hotels and living expenses if you cannot live in your home due to a covered event, while the repairs are being made.

E. Personal Liability Protection – covers you, covered family members and covered pets that you may own from lawsuits due to injury or property damage. Note with regard to pets, some insurance companies exclude some animals and breeds that are considered aggressive such as Pit Bull Terriers, etc.

F. Medical Payments (or MedPay) – helps cover medical expenses for someone injured on your property that does not result in a lawsuit.

RENTERS INSURANCE

As the renter of a home, you truly don't need to worry about insuring the home or structure of the building that you live in. That is for the landlord to worry about. What you do, however, need to worry about, is your personal belongings located in the property from theft or damage. Many renters assume that this coverage is covered under the landlord's insurance policy. This is incorrect. Renters insurance is usually remarkably inexpensive to have, and yet extremely crucial to have the coverage necessary to cover all that you possess. It is particularly pertinent to have adequate insurance if you have a lot of high value items. Remember to check with your insurance agent if you have large amounts of jewelry, guns, artwork, etc. as they may need individual riders. A rider provides extra protection above the standard protection covered under your standard insurance policy.

DWELLING INSURANCE

Dwelling Insurance is pretty self-explanatory. It covers the rebuilding or repairing of your dwelling (walls, structures, roof, etc.) in the event of a covered loss such as fire, hail, hurricane & lightening. Other separate policies may be needed for flood and earthquake insurance. This type of insurance policy is usually incorporated as Part A of a standard Homeowners Insurance Policy but can also be sold separately for people who are not living in a property themselves. People that might be most interested in this type of coverage would be a landlord as part of a Landlord Policy or a person with a second home. These policies are usually more expensive because you as the homeowner are not going to be in residence to upkeep or protect the home as you would if you lived there. Check around for the best deal but sometimes you can get discounts if you have multiple homes on the same insurance policy so you might begin by checking with the insurance agent you use for your primary home. If, for any reason, the home will remain vacant, make sure that you let the insurance agent know this. Sometimes a claim for certain types of damage will be denied if they occur on a vacant home. The last thing you want is to have a claim and not be able to get the help you have been paying for because of a misunderstanding. Always tell your insurance agent what you need and make sure you check the coverage provided, as well as the price (premium), BEFORE you buy.

FLOOD INSURANCE

Flood Insurance or a NFIP Policy (National Flood Insurance Policy) is a type of coverage that can be purchased on almost any home but it is extremely valuable coverage to have in the event you live in a flood plain or low lying area. If you do live in one of these areas, you will also more than likely be required, by your lender, to keep Flood Insurance on the property to cover them against loss. Keep in mind when purchasing a Flood Insurance Policy they usually have a waiting period so that people do not just call to get one when they are expecting a catastrophic flood event in their area. Price for premiums can vary like any other type of insurance policy, it is based on risk. If you are in an area that is more prone to flooding, than your premium will be higher. The pricing is based on Flood Zone Level. It is something to keep in mind if you are about to purchase a home though. If you have several homes to choose from, that you like, and one requires flood insurance based on where the home is located, it will cost you thousands of dollars extra to own that home over the period you own the home. Research the cost for the insurances BEFORE you buy, as this type of insurance will increase your monthly payments.

Below is the link to the Federal Emergency Management (FEMA) – FLOOD ZONE DEFINITIONS website for more explanations on flood prone areas.

https://msc.fema.gov/webapp/wcs/stores/servlet/info?storeId=10001&catalogId=10001&langId=-1&content=floodZones&title=FEMA%2520Flood%2520Zone%2520Designations

TAXES – THE TAX MAN COMETH

We as American Citizens (and other countries) have to pay taxes as part of our part of being a productive and prosperous society. The money that we pay as individuals, benefits all. The money raised is spent for things such as schools, police departments, fire departments, roads & highways and other things that help our families and our neighbors. Depending on the state you live in, there are various taxes that we may pay: Federal Income Tax, State Income Tax, Property Taxes, Personal Property Tax, State Sales Tax, etc. It is always important to pay your fair share, but I think most of us will agree that we don't want to pay more than our fair share. For every dollar that we do pay in taxes, it leaves one less for our budget. That being said, there are a couple of things that we can do to make sure it is less of a hardship when April 15th (the date when you must file your taxes in the U.S.) rolls around for your Federal Income Taxes.

HAVE THE RIGHT AMOUNT OF DEDUCTIONS TAKEN OUT

Many companies across the nation take Federal Income Tax out of your paycheck each pay period. When you start working, you will probably be asked to fill out a W4 Form. The W4 Form is a worksheet that helps employers have the information to take out the right amount from your paycheck for Federal Taxes. On the W4 form, for each allowance that you claim, the LESS money will be taken out of your paycheck. This sounds all fine and dandy EXCEPT if you do not have the right amount of taxes withheld, you may have an enormous surprise come April 15th when you find that you could owe hundreds or thousands to the Internal Revenue Service (IRS). I will float this idea to you right now to save you this grief. Try to have the LEAST amount of allowances possible. If you do it this way, instead of owing a large debt you could end up getting money back at tax time. That money could be used for something you want or need. You could even put some into your bank account. You could consider it like a forced savings plan. You will have a little less each pay period to spend, but if done correctly, you should get a substantial amount of money back at the end of the year.

FILE YOUR FEDERAL TAXES FOR FREE

 About eight or ten years ago I went to the IRS Website and followed a link where you could get your taxes done online for free. I went to this site and did indeed file my taxes for free with no hitches. I have been doing so for years and have told family and friends, who have also been happy with this service. You can go on there, day or night, 24 hours a day and follow the step by step instructions. It will tell you as you go through the steps, how much you owe or how much your refund will be based on the information you entered. I chose to have the refund direct deposited and about ten days later it went into my account. You can also choose several other refund options at the end.

 While this might not be for those that have very complicated tax returns, for the average person, it is an excellent opportunity to save sometimes hundreds of dollars. I even tested it out one time and went to a well-known National Tax Service to compare on a year that I thought would be more complicated. I asked them how much it would be to have them prepare my taxes. The tax preparer said they could not tell me until they finished, but it would be no obligation if I had the time. After about an hour, they came up with a refund of X. They wanted to charge me $250 which was sticker shock to a man that had been getting his taxes done for free for the last four or five years. I thanked them for their time but said no. I went home and did my taxes on the free site. Do you know what? It came out to the EXACT PENNY as the one that wanted to charge me $250. Give it a try if you want. You can fill out the information to test and see if you come up with what you think is the correct amount. After you are done, you can choose not to file your taxes through the service if you feel you are not satisfied. .

The website link that I use is below. There may be other web sites that will do this for free. I figured if the IRS suggested it as a preferred provider, than they must feel pretty confident in this free service. It was good enough for me. I have been a happy customer ever since. Good luck and good saving!

http://www.taxactonline.com/

COLLEGE CHOICES AND TUITION

Once again, I am not going to spend a considerable amount of time on this subject as there have been many entire books written about various aspects of college tuition and resources. Suffice it to say that you need to research very carefully BEFORE you sign up for anything. Obviously the bottom line is to get the best education at the lowest possible cost. To prepare that young man or woman with boundless dreams and energy, to go off to college, there are a couple of things you should consider.

• First and foremost, what college or colleges do they want to attend?

• What are the costs of those institutions? – see link in the next section below.

• Will your student qualify for any grants?

• Will your student be getting any scholarship funds?

IN STATE COLLEGE VERSUS OUT OF STATE COLLEGE-

Did you know that someone that lives in a state, and goes to a college in that same state, can save anywhere from two to three times the tuition cost what a person that lives in another state would pay to come to the same college. This is true with most state colleges and universities. They in essence give discounts to students from their own states. This reduces the competition from many students from other states that would normally apply. It also tells you that you need to make some decisions on what colleges you or universities that you are interested in attending and what you can afford.

Below is a fabulous link from CNN MONEY: How much will that college really cost? It is a very useful tool for parents and students to check and see what today's cost of college tuition, room and board, and books would be at the colleges you are interested in attending. It gives a state by state breakdown of the cost of a both In State and Out-of-State costs involved.

http://cgi.money.cnn.com/tools/collegecost/collegecost.html

PRIVATE COLLEGE VERSUS PUBLIC COLLEGE

It is best to decide on what you are interested in when it comes to a college that you want to attend and what you can afford. There are two main types of colleges:

PUBLIC COLLEGES - are largely supported by state funds. These colleges tend to be less expensive, especially if you are a resident of that state. Some states also have reciprocal agreements with local states allowing them the lower In State rates. It is always best to ask. Many state run schools are enormous and have a wide choice of majors to choose from. They also tend to have larger class sizes. I have heard more they also have more red tape as there are many people clamoring to be accepted.

PRIVATE COLLEGES – are mostly supported by tuition, endowment and donations from former alumni. Usually these colleges are more expensive than the public colleges. In general, they have far fewer choices in curriculums and majors to choose from but can make up for this by having smaller class sizes and easier access to professors. Obviously this will change from school to school.

FEDERAL PELL GRANT PROGRAM

The Federal Pell Grant Program is a Federal Grant, unlike a loan, and does not need to be repaid. The maximum Pell Grant award for the 2011-2012 year if $5,550. Each year, the Pell Grant amount can change, so I thought this was a resource that should be brought out in this book. You can go to the U.S. Department of Education's web site to find out more about the Federal Pell Grant Program. You can also apply at their web site.

http://www2.ed.gov/programs/fpg/index.html

HAVE YOU CONSIDERED A RENTAL PROPERTY?

Have you ever thought what you will do about the cost of room and board for your young student? Have you ever considered looking into buying a home or rental property in the college town that your child will attend for college? Look into the costs and see if you could easily rent out other rooms in the house to other students looking to live off campus.

In addition, it could mean enormous savings on your college tuition itself: An Out-Of-State college student can pay two to three times what an In State student would pay. Check with your college and see what the stipulations are for being considered an "In State" student. They usually require having lived in the state that the college is located in for a period of time. Keep this in mind when you go to purchase the home or rental property. If you own a home there and the student lives in residence at that home, you should be able to qualify for and prove that they have an in state residency.

Look into the potential tax benefits of owning a rental property and if you feel you could meet, interview and handle the leases and any issues that may arise. It might be a reasonable thing to consider. Keep in mind, the safety of your student and consistent payment flow from the other tenants in the home, to offset the costs, should be some key issues to consider if you decide you are interested in this. With your son or daughter living in the home, you may get Homeowners Insurance discounts also as a second home. Be honest and let the Insurance Agent know that you intend on renting out a room or two for extra money but have a family member in residence. See what the agent can do for you. A couple of other things that could influence your decision are:

• What are rooms renting for locally?

• How many rooms could you rent out?

• What would be your mortgage payment?

• Would you be able to cover the excess if the rooms were not all rented out?

• Would you be able to get any tax breaks and possibly pay your child to be an onsite manager handling any issues that arose?

For the right person and the right family, you could end up having your child's room and board paid for while hopefully gaining equity in the property at the same time. With interest rates being at nearly historic lows, it could make a great deal of sense.

PREPAID COLLEGE PROGRAMS

This may be one possible way to pay for tomorrow's education at today's prices. Check with your local state and see if they offer a Pre-paid College Program. If they do, you may be able to choose a plan that encompasses what you think you can afford and what your child will need. Once set up, you make payments to the plan's administrator until they become college age. This allows you to build up a college fund to cover a majority of the expenses for the tuition plan chosen in advance over many years. Make sure to ask what happens in the event that your child decides they do not want to go to college. Some of these programs will either refund the entire amount that you put into the program (without the interest accrued) or transfer the plan to a sibling or grandchild of your choosing.

In addition to the individual states, there are some other options. The link below has a group of colleges from across the United States that participate in a pre-paid college format. Check and see if the colleges that you would be interested in your child attending are on the list. It's an excellent place to start.

https://www.privatecollege529.com/OFI529/

TAX BENEFITS FOR EDUCATION

Take advantage of the tax credits offered for educational expenses. That's what they are there for. At the time of the writing of this book (2012), under just one of these tax breaks, The American Opportunity Tax Credit is worth up to $2500 to those that qualify and receive income less than $180,000 annually. There are also additional tax deductions for things like Student Loan Interest and others.

Please follow the link below to access the Internal Revenue Centers (IRS) information on the various tax credits that are available for education. This list can change yearly, so keep this link for the most up to date information available straight from the IRS.

http://www.irs.gov/newsroom/article/0,,id=213044,00.html

CABLE, SATELLITE OR ANTENNAE
Which Is Best For You?

When assessing what is the best entertainment package for you, there are a few things to consider. Think about what your financial goals are. Keeping that in mind, how relevant is television to you and your family? Look at what shows and TV Channels are most pertinent to you and if you can stream reruns at the TV Networks own channel. If you live in or near a major metropolitan area, you may have a lot of options to consider. On the other hand, if you live in a more rural area, far from locally broadcasted stations that would normally come through the air, than you may have fewer options. Below are a couple questions to consider.

1.) Do you have high speed internet accessible in your area? If so, could you use your computer or an internet connected device to stream movies and programming to your television?

2.) Are you able to pick up locally broadcasted television stations through the air via a Digital TV Converter Box? These boxes usually range $50 - $100 and will pick up broadcast stations in your local area, if you are in the range of the stations. Many TV's have their own converters built into the televisions and can pick up and convert the video stream without purchasing an additional set top box. Try hooking your TV up to a standard, set top antennae (rabbit ears) or outside antennae and go to you menu. Search for channels using air/cable and see how many channels you pick up. You can also check and see with your neighbors if they are able to get decent TV reception from their homes before purchasing a bunch of equipment if you prefer.

CABLE OR SATELLITE COMPANIES

Many cable and satellite companies will offer you a special "introductory rate" package if you sign up for a period of time. It is advantageous for them, because you commit to a longer period of time (usually one or two years). For that commitment, they will give you a discounted rate for the television programming package that is relevant to you. Be extremely careful with this though. Many of these packages have penalty fees if you decide to move and cannot transfer your package to where you are moving. Make sure to ask BEFORE you sign up what charges are involved in set up. Also make sure to find out if there are any penalty fees that you would be responsible for if you decide that the package is not right for you or stopped purchasing the package. Try to get a package that has no penalties or commitments. I will tell you that most things are negotiable. If there are certain fees that you do not feel you should pay for, ask the Customer Service Representative if they would waive the fee for you or what they can do to offset the fees. If they can waive the installation fee or give you some other perk to help offset the charge, you are that much better off.

COMBINE TO SAVE MONEY

Many cable companies will offer combo rates to you. They call it bundling. These packages can include high speed internet, cable and cable telephone at a discounted combo rate for a certain time period (usually a one or two year commitment). If you use all three of these services, and it makes sense then go ahead and take advantage of the offer. After this period of time ends, the pricing will increase. You can always call Customer Service and ask them what specific deals they can offer you at that time. Make sure to ask for the Retention Department as they are the ones that have the best deals available to help keep you as a customer. You might mention that you saw a competitive cable company or satellite company that was offering an exceptional deal and see if they can match it.

I saw a major telephone company getting into this action by offering their own package of high speed internet, unlimited local and long distance telephone and a satellite TV company as the combo package discount. Once again, do these services and packages meet your budget and your expectations for what you want? If so then take advantage of the offer.

CABLE MODEMS & EQUIPMENT

Did you know that you may be able to purchase some of your cable company's equipment instead of renting it? That's always better in my book, if its reasonable priced and the dollars make sense. After a period of time, (a year or two) some cable companies are willing to sell you some of their equipment as they are always upgrading equipment.

An example of this, I called my cable/internet company and asked the Customer Service Representative if there was anything I could do to reduce my bill. They were kind enough to let me know that for $30.00, I could purchase the cable modem that I was renting from them for $5.00 per month. I figured it had lasted nearly two years already without a hitch while I was renting it and if the modem lasted longer than six months then I would be ahead of the game. It has now been over two years. The modem is still going strong. Those little things add up to hefty savings in the long run. That's a savings of $90 and counting after the equipment was paid for.

The thing about high tech electrical equipment like modems, routers, computers, TV, radios, etc. is, if they are going to have a problem, it will probably happen soon after you purchase or start using them. If they last the first year without an issue, they will generally continue to work well for many years to come, They will probably last until the technology becomes nearly antiquated. Think of how many people have the monstrous older model TV's in their home. Even with the advent of flat screen and cable ready TV's many of these still keep turning on and giving excellent service. One last thought on this subject is that if I had not asked the Customer Service Representative than I would have never known.

HIGH SPEED INTERNET

The internet can be amazing. There are answers to almost any question to be had on the internet. I wish that it was available when I was growing up. The internet community is astonishing, many people are willing to share the information that they know best either through a blog that they do or You Tube videos. There are millions of web sites and fascinating tidbits that you can find about the most obscure or popular interests that you might have, and all you need to pay for the price of admission is a monthly fee to access the internet and have a computer or internet accessible device.

To make it even less expensive, there are wi-fi hot spots that make wireless internet access to their customers. Some businesses such as restaurants, coffee shops and hotels to name a few offer free access to wi-fi internet while you are using their establishments. You can go to these places and enjoy a meal or a pleasant night's rest while doing anything from work to web surfing at no additional charge. Keep an eye out at the places that you frequent and look for signs on the door or just ask if you are unsure. Free ALWAYS fits in my book! I am sure that it will in yours also.

All internet access is not created equal. The Internet Service Provider (ISP) that you choose to pay to have your internet service through will affect how quickly you can move about the World Wide Web (Internet). To access the internet, your computer uploads and downloads small bits of information called bytes. The speed that these bytes are able to be uploaded (upload speed) and downloaded (download speed) is called bandwidth. Ask your prospective Internet Service Provider what bandwidth you are going to be paying for your internet service. The faster the upload speeds and particularly download speeds, the faster you will be able to access your favorite sites. Keep in mind, they may quote you those famous words "UP TO" a certain speed so you might want to clarify with them what the minimum speeds that you can expect.

Some of the types of internet access that may find that is available for your home or office is:

• Dial Up – This is usually very slow, good for basic email and slow web crawling.

• DSL – A connection that is always on and available, run through your existing telephone lines. This can be very good for email, fast web access, streaming video and gaming. There may be various speeds and pricing structures.

• Cable Modem – A broadband internet connection through your existing cable lines, accessed by using a Cable Modem. Usually very fast web access, good for email, streaming video and gaming. There may be various speeds and pricing structures.

• Wireless Internet Connections – Many smart phones and cell phones as well as I-pods, Kindle's, laptops, e-readers etc. can access the internet using wireless internet connection within the device and connected via a wireless network. This is generally more expensive service if you are paying for access anywhere and mainly its available in more metropolitan areas. This is not the wireless internet that is connected through a router run through your own home network although many of these devices can also access those home networks if you are within range of the router.

• Satellite – You access the internet through a modem that is connected via satellite. Due to the extreme distances that the date needs to go both to and from the satellite it is usually much slower than some of the other options but if you are in an area that this is the only option you may consider it.

STREAMING VIDEO FROM THE WEB

With the advent of high speed internet connections, it leaves you the consumer, with a wide array of free video options that are part of the ever changing internet landscape. Many things are free. Some are at extremely low cost for the quality and amount of streaming video content that you have the choice of enjoying.

ROKU - This is a wonderful little TV or desktop device that measures only about 4" square. You can purchase from major department stores or even online at their own website roku.com. The prices range from about $50 to $100 as a onetime fee. The pricing is based on the quality that you want to be able to see. I purchased the $99.00 one that will accept full 1080 HD. In only a few minutes you can be perusing through potentially hundreds of channels, all of which are currently available If that's not enough for you, you can search the internet for a list of private channels for ROKU. These are channels that are made up by independent sources, and many have the access code to enter online at ROKU to add to your channel lineup.

All of the channels are available On Demand where you can start and stop them to meet your busy schedule. Most are channels that are either little or no charge. There are channels that encompass everything from free movies, music, news and weather to specialty items such as cooking, gardening, hunting, fishing, beauty, fitness, entertainment and gaming. It is an absolutely awesome little device. There is so much free content, you could literally watch 24 hours per day. They even have a ROKU now that makes your remote control a video game controller where you can play games over your ROKU. One of the best bets for the money in my book!

FREE CONTENT ON THE WEB – There is a HUGE amount of free content that you can access on the internet through your computer or web friendly TV. Many of the Broadcasters such as ABC, NBC, CBS, and FOX make their shows available for free in an On-Demand format. The easiest way to find out if your favorite TV shows are available for streaming is to do an internet search with the title that you are using and use key words "Full Episode". Be wary of your search results and look at the web addresses that come up to see if they are reputable websites. Some of the best sites I have found are youtube.com and crackle.com but there are tons and tons of others, just let your fingers do the walking. Enjoy!

THE ELECTRIC & GAS UTILITIES
How Can You Save Money?

REDUCING YOUR CONSUMTION

The easiest way to save something is not to use it in the first place. As you are examining how to lower your debt and becoming more self-sufficient when dealing with your money, it is also an opportune time to look at what you can save on your electric and gas bills. These are one of those bills that you have to work into your budget and pay like clockwork. We all need electric and/or gas to run everything from our appliances to keep our food fresh to keeping our homes warm or cool depending on the time of year. It also helps power up the devices for your fun time like video game systems, stereos and Televisions.

GET A FREE HOME ENERGY SURVEY

Contact your local electric company and see if they will provide a free Home Energy Survey for your home. Many times they will send someone out to check your home and show possible problem areas as well as give you suggestions and tips on how to reduce your energy consumption and your carbon footprint.

Below is a link to the U.S. Department of Energy's website that can help with saving money on a variety of energy saving ways. If you click on the Home Energy Saver auditing tool, it can help you conduct your own energy assessment:

http://www.energysavers.gov/seasonal/energy_assessment.html

The main web site to explore the other ways of saving for your home or apartment:

http://www.energysavers.gov/

SOME OF THE BEST ENERGY SAVING TIPS FOR YOUR HOME

CHANGE OUT YOUR LIGHT BULBS – Make an investment that makes sense. That's right, use those light bulbs that look like plugged in electric curly fries. Did you know that those curly fluorescent light bulbs are beneficial for your pocketbook and also the world? That's right, they use up to 75% less energy and can last up to 10 times longer than the old style incandescent light, all this while giving off the same brightness of light that you are used to. I know these light bulbs cost you a dollar or two more when you buy them, but look at the savings that you will enjoy over time. Keep in mind that according to the energystar.gov website that tracks such energy efficiencies each light bulb, can save you up to $130 over its lifetime. I am all for paying for things that SAVE me money.

HANG YOUR CLOTHES OUT TO DRY – The top three energy hog appliances in your home are, your dish washer, refrigerator and clothes dryer. You can of course hand wash and dry your dishes of course. This uses less water and no electricity. You can even wash your dishes by hand and use your dish washer as a drying rack. This makes even more sense. With your refrigerator, you can make sure that it is level and the door seals well, so that you are not losing energy from the seals. This brings us to the last of the big three and probably the biggest energy hog, your clothes dryer. You can of course decide not to wash your clothes, but your friends and family will of course get tired of wearing a clothes pin on their nose when talking to you. If you have the space, you can set up the old fashioned clothes line if you are lucky enough to have bright, sunny weather. That's right, it worked for our ancestors and is standard in many parts of the world, there is no reason that you can't take that plunge and air dry your clothes. You certainly can save money.

The last thing I want to say about your appliances is to look, when you replace them, at the Energy Star rating system that you will find on modern appliances. Look to purchase the one that has the best energy rating that you can afford.

USE SMART POWER STRIPS – These are power strips that you can either purchase online or at your local hardware store that will reduce "leaking electricity" and standby power. Did you realize that most of our modern appliances have standby power and "leak energy". This means that they are actually on but only using partial power waiting for you to click a button and them to come on instantaneously. The reason they don't have to warm up is that they keep themselves warmed up ALL OF THE TIME, even when not being used. These smart strips are excellent. They have different colored plug ins. There is one main plug that is the trigger. When you turn on that appliance, the other devices plugged in will also have power to them. This is perfect for areas such as setting up your TV as the trigger. When you turn on your TV or trigger device, you also will have power to the VCR, Game Console, DVD player, etc. Look at it this way. You won't use the Game Console without having the Television on. You can think of lots of places in your home that you might be able, not only to save money, but also to save wear and tear on your small appliances so you don't have to replace them as often. This is a win/win in my book. Who knew? The other thing that you can do is simply unplug unused appliances and gadgets, including your cell phone and digital camera battery chargers. Anything plugged in will generally be using electricity.

LOW INCOME HOME ENERGY ASSISTANCE PROGRAM (LIHEAP)

The Low Income Home Energy Assistance Programs primary goal is to help low income families that pay a high percentage of their family income for home energy to be able to meet their immediate home energy needs.

A grant is given to each state yearly and is distributed to those that are assessed as needing it the most from those that apply.

What types of assistance does LIHEAP provide?
- Bill payment assistance
- Energy crisis assistance
- Weatherization and energy-related home repairs

To find out more information on what monies are available and if you qualify you can go to the link below at the U.S. Department of Children & Families:

http://www.acf.hhs.gov/programs/ocs/liheap/

FREE FIREWOOD AND MULCH

Did you know that many of the local landfills offer free firewood as well as free mulch? This will help the environment by reducing the amount of waste that needs to get buried in the landfills as well as your pocketbook if you happen to have a fireplace or wood burning stove for heating during the winter. I know the mulch is not used for energy consumption. I thought I would mention it here because it's still good for your budget and you can help beautify your home for a little sweat equity (work). Call your local landfill or waste removal service and see what they offer and the location that you can pick it up.

One other place to get excellent free firewood is if you see a construction company clearing a lot or large plot of land. Come back near quitting time and bring your truck and a chainsaw. Ask for the building contractor/site supervisor or who is in charge and ask him/her if they would mind if you cut some firewood from the trees that they had cleared. At least these trees are already dropped to the ground. They will probably have the bulldozers push them up in a pile and burn them so it's less work for them. This also gives you the option of choosing the firewood (hickory, oak, etc.) and tree size that you want to work with. Make sure to thank the Foreman who gives you permission.

Another place you can check for free firewood is an organization that looks to help the environment by reducing landfill waste on things that can be recycled is called Freecycle.org. They are a group of like-minded individuals who offer things to others in the organization for free. If you don't see firewood offered on there, you can actually place a wanted ad on the website asking if any members have a tree that you can remove or one they have cut down already that you can haul away for firewood. You can help them, and they can help you. It's a terrific organization. The website address is below. To sign up, you need to request to become a member.

www.freecycle.org

One last place to check for free firewood and many other free things you can check with the Craigslist website from your local area. Under "For Sale", there is a FREE category where people will list things they are getting rid of at no charge. Check it out here:

www.craigslist.org

WIRED, WIRELESS OR INTERNET PHONE - WHAT WORKS FOR YOU?

In today's day and age of wireless cell phones a lot of people are giving up their land lines. Here are a couple of things to consider:

• WHAT KIND OF BUDGET DO YOU HAVE? – This is extremely important. I know someone who has an internet phone through www.magicjack.com. The magicjack is advertised at approximately $50 to purchase the device, then its $19.95 per year. She is very pleased with it. The thing with internet phones is, they run through your internet and your computer so if you have an emergency unless your computer is on, it may take a couple of minutes to turn the computer and boot up the internet phone. However, if this is a home phone you use when needed and have a cell phone where you can pre-purchase minutes like www.tracfone.com, it might be a potent combination. You may end up spending far less than you would spend on monthly plans. See how much you have to spend in your budget and see the best deals you can work out to meet your needs.

• HOW MANY PHONES WILL YOU NEED? – If you drop the land line, what happens if you leave to go somewhere and take the phone? Will your spouse and children need additional phones? If so, how many. How much would a multiple cell phone plan cost you?

• WHAT IF YOU LOSE YOUR ELECTRIC? – Your land line or internet phone will not work. Your cell phone will work (if charged).

• WHAT KIND OF PACKAGES CAN YOU GET? – Check with your carrier and shop around, see the best deals and bundles that you can get. Make sure to read everything extremely carefully. You may be able to package cable phone, internet and cable together so that it works out that you get the landline with unlimited Long Distance for nearly free.

• WHAT ABOUT 911 SERVICE? – If you call on a land line, the local 911 service is called. They have your address and can respond, even without you letting them know your address. This gives you a great deal of peace of mind. If you call from a cell phone or internet based phone, it will not be linked to your address. You will have to tell the 911 operator where you are. (NOTE: With an internet based phone that you use from home or office, you can contact your local police departments and tie your internet phone number to your address)

• END UNWANTED SALES CALLS – Did you know the government created and has been running a "Do Not Call List" since June of 2003. You can register your home, business or cell phone number on this list. By doing so, most telemarketers are subject to substantial fines if they call you to solicit or sell you goods or services if you lodge a complaint against them and they are found to be in violation. Remember that charities, political parties and surveyors are not covered, but it will reduce a great many of these unwanted sales calls. It's a remarkably simple process. To sign up for the National Do Not Call Registry go to:

https://www.donotcall.gov/

BE CAREFUL, ASK ABOUT DATA LIMITS FOR WIRELESS PHONES

With the advent of 3G and 4G wireless telephones, they have apps that allow you to do everything from stream videos and play games to surf the internet. Make sure to find out if the carrier that you choose has the right plan for you. If you don't, you could be in for a big surprise. If you use too much data, some of the national carriers will "Throttle" your phone, or slow it down so slow that you will be forced to quit downloading data or muddle through at such extremely slow speeds that you will be totally exasperated. Assess how you use your cell phone/smart phone every month and see which carrier offers a plan that fits your budget and your needs.

At the time of this writing, Sprint claims to be the only national wireless cell phone carrier that offers truly unlimited data transfers, unlimited texting and unlimited calling from any mobile phone in America for one monthly fee. Seems like a good place to start your research:

http://community.sprint.com/baw/community/sprintblogs/announcements/blog/2012/05/17/sprint-is-only-national-wireless-carrier-offering-truly-unlimited-data-for-smartphones

PC World did an excellent article on VoIP phones that are internet phones. You can read it as part of your research if you are interested below:

http://www.pcworld.com/article/118734/is_an_internet_phone_right_for_you.html

ARE FREE CELL PHONES AND PERKS REALLY FREE?

There is an old saying, nothing is ever truly free. This is something to keep in mind. With many cell phone plans, you are required to sign up for an extended period of time (2 years is typical). This locks you in to X amount per month for that period of time. The wireless carriers have to build the price of these high dollar phones into their plans. This is how they offer them to you at such reduced prices or even free. Those FREE phones are being paid for out of the expected monthly payments. If you end up canceling the plan early, you will probably be responsible for significant penalties that can cost you hundreds of dollars. Make sure to ask if there are any penalties if you cancel your plan early BEFORE you sign up for a plan. One primary place to start deciding on a plan or carrier is to ask family and friends what carrier they have and what plan and if they are happy with their service. Ask them if they are getting what they are paying for. This can help alleviate all of the pain of getting the wrong carrier and plan and being stuck paying for years on something that you are not happy with.

HOW TO AVOID "BILL SHOCK"

Have you ever opened your cell phone bill and found that your $49.00 plan was all of a sudden $250? No. Well, you are lucky. I can tell you, it happens to a lot more people than you might think. Sometimes those bills are much, much higher. It is imperative that you KNOW WHAT YOUR PLAN INCLUDES. More importantly, find out what charges are assessed to your bill if you go over the plans allotments.

I know a man who was the lucky recipient of one of these bills when his then 16 year old daughter had almost a twenty page bill of texts at 10 cents per text. They did not have unlimited texting, and he had asked her not to use the phone for texting. The daughter said she would not, but later thought she would just pay the difference and began texting with her friends.

An entire month went by and at the end of the month they both got a hefty surprise. The thing was, they could have purchased unlimited texting at the time for an additional $10.00 per month. To her credit, she did pay the bill. He made a call to the carrier and asked them if he could add the $10.00 per month to their plan and reduce the $180 texts charge. The cell phone carrier refused to do anything for the man and counted their profits.

He asked when his plan was set to renew so that he could cancel and found it was about four months in the future. To cancel early, it would have been a $200 penalty per phone or $400 for nothing. He decided to keep the plan until the end of his commitment. He marked the day on the calendar and circled it in red. That day he called and cancelled the plan with a big smile on his face. He went out and purchased a pre-paid cell phone (www.tracfone.com) with double minutes for life for $29.00 at Walmart. Now he saves hundreds of dollars per year without long term commitments. He is now smiling all the way to the bank. The wireless carrier has lost a customer and will never get a dime from the man again.

YOUR WATER BILL

WHEN LOOKING FOR A HOME – LOOK FOR ONE WITH A WELL

The easiest way to save money on your water bill is not to have one! When you are seeking to purchase or rent a home, look for a home that is on a well if you have the opportunity. There are several reasons. Obviously not having an extra bill every month is a tremendous benefit. If you are on a well with clean water all you pay for is the minimal amount of energy it costs to run the pump, to pump the water to the surface.

If you live on land or have the space for a garden, this will help maximize your savings. It allows you to have an abundant water supply for your home and also have water for a garden. Having a garden is a marvelous thing. Kids and families can have fun working together tilling, planting and harvesting nature's bounty by making a garden of any size. In addition, they will make life lessons. You can have a variety of delicious vegetables of myriad varieties.

You can even use containers or use square foot gardening if you don't have a large piece of property. There are tons of videos on www.youtube.com, where people will share their knowledge and show you exactly how to plant a garden and help grow your own food. Your kids will also get extraordinary life lessons on where the food comes from that ends up on your table and you will save money on the grocery bill.

TIPS AT REDUCING YOUR WATER USAGE

The next way to save money, if you do have a water bill every month, is to reduce your water usage. When you are paying by the gallon, every bit you save will be a help. As water becomes more expensive and is in shorter supply in the future, the savings will only multiply.

RAIN BARREL – Get a large rain barrel or you can even create multiple rain barrels. If you have a downspout that comes off of the gutter system, from your roof, you would be amazed at how quickly a 50 gallon barrel will fill up. To make it easy access you can even drill and attach a garden hose fitting low on the barrel and use for watering your plants and garden.

PLACE A BRICK IN YOUR TOILET TANK – Did you know that you can place a brick or even a sand filled plastic bottle into the tank of your toilet and each time you flush your toilet you will use that much less water. Multiply that many flushes times how many bathrooms you have. That is quite a substantial savings.

WATER YOUR LAWN NOT YOUR SIDEWALKS AND STREET– When you water your lawn and set up your sprinklers to get the maximum amount of coverage without duplicating where you just watered and try to avoid concrete & wasted areas. This will give you the water where you need it with the least amount of waste.

WATER GRASS & GARDEN EARLY IN THE MORNING – The best time to water your lawn and garden is between 4AM and 9AM before the sun burns off everything you are trying to get to the roots of your plants. When you water in the morning, you want to soak the soil at the roots real well, so that the plants will send out strong, deep roots. The deeper the roots of the plant, the less you have to water them because they are able to draw up the water from the ground below where it is cooler. If you water your plants in the evening, you could have too much moisture hanging there overnight. This can create things like Fungus or Root Rot.

WATER CONTAINERS AND PROBLEM AREAS BY HAND – If you are trying to reach one corner of the yard that is hard to set up a sprinkler or have containers use a hose or watering can. You can place the water exactly where you want it and use just the correct amount you need. This is much better than trying to set up a sprinkler to reach the small areas, and having most of the water go into the patio or street, etc.

CHECK FAUCETS, SPIGOTS AND TOILETS FOR LEAKS – Check your faucets and spigots for drips and leaks. You would be amazed at how much water can seep away drip by drip. If you find a leak, you can either, tighten, fix or replace the fixture. Many times it can be something as uncomplicated as a small rubber gasket. Check you hose connections on outside hoses and make sure the connections don't spray or leak so that all of the water you use is where you want it. One final suggestion, make sure your toilet is not running. This can make an enormous difference on your water bill. If you see water constantly trickling down into the toilet bowl, then you need to make an adjustment in the flapper or interior plunger inside the water tank.

You can go to the link below to get 100 additional tips on conserving water. They have some brilliant ideas:

http://wateruseitwisely.com/100-ways-to-conserve/

LOCAL CITY GOVERNMENT

Did you know that many parts of your local city government are happy to offer some helpful and valuable things to their local citizens. Just a few examples are listed below:

POLICE DEPARTMENT – The police department is your local community is there "To Serve and Protect" and these dedicated men and women take their job extremely seriously. Check with your local police department and see if they offer any of the following as I have seen police departments offer through the years.

• FREE TRIGGER GUARDS FOR FIREARMS – To help keep our children safe.

• STEERING WHEEL LOCKS – (For Certain Models) To help reduce auto theft.

• FREE CHILD CAR SEATS – Once again to help keep our children safe.

• SAFETY HELMETS AND REFLECTORS FOR BIKES -

FIRE DEPARTMENT – These outstanding men and women who run into fires when everyone else is running out of one are also on the job to help the community. I have seen many local fire departments give away at no charge Smoke Detectors for your home to help you and your family in the event of a fire. As the survivor of a home fire, I know the importance of what a smoke detector can do. These outstanding men and women who are our hero's.

LOCAL LANDFILLS – May offer free firewood and mulch as explained earlier.

GOVERNMENT OWNED AUCTIONS – Below is the link to the national database of government owned surplus and seizures that are sold at auction. Check out this website. It is chalk full of cars, trucks, boats, computers, etc. to name only a few, owned by the government. Good luck and good savings!

http://www.govsales.gov/govsales/govsales/#

STORES AND GROCERY STORES

With the advent of the internet has certainly changed things out there in the retail and food stores playing field. We have seen some of the largest box stores such as Circuit City close their doors because of the increased competition. For the consumer, it has made things easier to gather information.

GO ONLINE TO YOUR LOCAL FOOD STORES WEBSITE TO SEE SALE PAPERS

Searching the internet can save you a lot of time. Most of the local grocery stores have their weekly sale papers online in today's day and age. This gives you the opportunity to see who has the products on sale that you want for the week or to stock up on. You can be prepared BEFORE you go to the store.

Did you know that you can save a tremendous amount of money by making a list of what you need before you get to the store and then sticking to that list? Grocers and retailers are savvy business people. Retail chains do studies on where to places colorful displays of foods, drinks and seasonal items to attract the most amount of attention and to get you to purchase items spur of the moment. Those items can cost you hundreds or even thousands of dollars over the period of a year. While it is gratifying to splurge every once in a while, you should know and keep tabs on what you are spending, or you will continue to the checkout counter and have an enormous surprise waiting for you when the clerk finishes ringing up your bill.

COUPONS – YOU DON'T NEED TO BE EXTREME – JUST SAVE!

I know many of you have all seen the TV shows and youtube.com videos on extreme couponing. These have brought a resurgence of interest, at a time, when we all need to get back to the basics of saving money on the things that we NEED to buy: food and household goods. It would be great to save those kinds of money. You would be able to get things for free or nearly free for your family, friends and community and as you can see from these videos it is possible. For those of you that do not have the time, energy or resources to put the effort into to get to that Superstar of Savings level, what you should take away from these shows are that ANYTHING IS POSSIBLE. A little homework goes a long way. Remember: Every time you save money on things you NEED to buy, that is money in your pocket to be used on something that you WANT TO USE BUY.

WHATS THE BEST DEAL? – Remember this, you are only saving money if you get a terrific deal on something that you will use and more importantly that it is something that you would use anyway. What I mean is this, if you have a coupon for 50 cents for a product that is normally priced $1.00 over the name brand you purchase then you are actually spending 50 cents MORE than you would normally pay. That is not the way to get rich. On the other hand, if you have that 50 cent coupon on that product that you enjoy and can never seem to fit into the budget and its Double Coupon Day, you can treat yourself and get that item for the same price as you would normally spend. Now the very best scenario is that you have a coupon for the product that you normally buy. You would actually save 50 cents ($1.00 if Double Coupon Day). That is what we want to aim for.

I will never forget a story we were once told by my instructor in Real Estate School. It went like this. What is the better deal, a fifty dollar dress that you use all the time, that you like the color, look and feel and wear it so much that it is nearly thread bare when you give up on it or a dress you purchase ON SALE for $20.00. You wear it one time and decide you don't like it or the color is not right for you, or it fits too snug, etc. It sits in your closet constantly being passed over until it ends up going to charity or a yard sale. The question is: Which was the better deal? The answer is of course the $50.00 dress because you wore it many, many times, so if you break down the cost per the time you wore and enjoyed it would be 50 cents (example 100 times) for each time you wore it. The $20.00 SALE dress cost you $20.00 for each time you wore it. This is an exceptionally strong economics lesson my friends.

CALL TO FIND THE STORES COUPON POLICY – As with anything, you need to follow the rules. Call the local grocery stores that you frequent and ask them what their coupon policy is. Some will direct you to a web site that you can print it out. Others may have a printed set of rules that they will give to you while you are in the store. See who offers the best deals.

FIND WHO OFFERS DOUBLE COUPON DAYS AND WHEN THEY ARE – While you are on the same phone call with the store about the coupon policy, ask them if they have double coupon days and when they are in the month so that you can maximize your savings.

CALL YOUR LOCAL NEWSPAPER – Find out when they have their manufacturer coupon days. Also, ask for the Circulation Department and ask them how much their subscription price is to get these newspapers to your door on those days. Ask if there are any discounted specials. Many times, newspapers will offer special pricing for new subscribers. Also, look at the newspaper boxes on the street and in your local store. See how much the cost of buying a regular newspaper would be on the days that have the coupons. You may find it might save you money just to purchase the individual newspapers.

FIND OUT WHICH STORE WILL PRICE MATCH – This is extremely valuable. If you have several local grocery stores that have sale papers and you are able to get all or most items at the same store by price matching (for the same items) then you save time, gasoline and money. That's a beautiful thing, I know that many of your local grocery stores will price match for the same brand product that they carry. This deal gets even sweeter if you have a manufactures coupon for the product (Double Coupon Day it and you are in heaven ladies and gentlemen)!

GREAT DEALS ON DAY OLD MEATS, BAKERY AND PRODUCE – One of the best things you can do for your food bill is to look in the bakery, meat and produce aisles for day old deals. The bakery deals are usually located on rolling carts in the bakery section of your supermarket. Whether you have a sweet tooth that just needs to be filled or want a great loaf of bread for spaghetti that night, you can begin by checking here. They are still fresh and wonderful but if not sold that day these items will be thrown away. As for the meats, these are discounted by up to fifty percent and would end up with a similar fate as the bakery items. These meats can be frozen or eaten within a day or two and have every bit the flavor, protein and nutrients at half the cost. As for the produce, I am sure you have probably seen these packages on wheeled carts in the produce section that are bundled together and in cellophane wrap, they may be slightly wilted or have some soft spots on them which can easily be cut off when in your kitchen. Take advantages of the savings when you can folks!

YARD SALES, CONSIGNMENT SHOPS AND CHARITIES

Folks let me tell you. You don't have to pay retail to look and feel terrific. Let someone else buy those name brand clothes and shoes and wear them in and then you as an educated consumer, can take advantage of picking them up at penny's on the dollar after they are nicely worn in and comfortable. All you need to make sure is that there are no stains or holes in the clothes or shoes, etc. Get home with them, throw them in your washer, and you are good to go.

Almost anything that you purchase goes down in value. If it is a long lasting item, you can save money by looking on Ebay or Craigslist or other websites like these online. You can also look in your local Goodwill or other charity second hand stores and consignment shops. This also works for furniture and household items. If you look hard enough, you can find a great deal on almost anything that you are searching for. While you need to be careful when looking on the internet for scams, with a little due diligence on your part, you can get an excellent deal and do wonders for your wallet at the same time.

LOOK ONLINE TO SAVE MONEY - Here's a tip for you that may help you weed out ads that you see on websites like Craigslist and other websites where you actually have to meet someone to purchase the product. This leaves you in a vulnerable position as you are bringing cash and you don't know the buyer.

ON HIGH DOLLAR ITEMS – Call the seller and tell them that you would be interested in seeing the car, boat or other item but that you will not be bringing cash. If all looks good, you would just ask that they follow you to your local bank to finalize the transaction. Your bank won't mind. Everyone will be more comfortable. It is a reasonable request. Any legitimate seller should be willing to grant this request if your bank is within a couple of miles. This way you are putting them on notice that will arrive with no money. Always meet in a public place where there will be other people around. You can also bring someone else with you for extra security if you like. Remember thieves want an easy mark, don't be that easy mark.

DO A REVERSE PHONE NUMBER LOOK UP – For those of you that do not know what a reverse phone number lookup is, you can go to the link below and type in the phone number from the seller in the add. If the phone is a land line and does not have an unlisted number, it will tell you who has that phone number and the person's name associated with the phone number and also their street address. If it's a mobile number, it will tell you. You have options to pay a small fee for the name associated with the mobile number. It's a powerful tool to help you if you only have a phone number to go by and want to avoid getting ripped off.

http://www.whitepages.com/reverse_phone/

NEWSPAPERS

With the advent of the internet, the role of newspapers in daily life has changed. Many newspapers are actually reducing or fighting to retain their printed newspaper products. Everyone wants to go online and find what they are searching for. The good news for you as a consumer is that most of the newspapers have online editions for FREE. Just by the click of a mouse you can jump from coast to coast in the blink of an eye and read almost any newspaper you want from your home town to the big city. Just get on your favorite search engine like Google, Bing or Yahoo and type in the newspaper you want to check out.

COUPONS - The one thing that you can't get online are the Coupons. Check with your local newspaper and see if they have any specials that you can take advantage of, to receive the papers that have the manufacturers coupons delivered to your home. Some time you need to spend a little money to make some and who doesn't like sitting down with a good cup of Coffee, Tea or Hot Chocolate and read that twenty pound Sunday Newspaper!

CLASSIFIED ADS – Once again if you are searching out a good deal on merchandise in your area, you can look either in the classified ad section of your local newspaper or even check them out online. It can be chock-full of fantastic deals.

DISCOUNTED AIRLINE TICKETS

ONLINE DISCOUNT TRAVEL SITES – There are some excellent travel sites that you can check online. Much like the hotel business the best way, to improve your bottom line if you're an airline, is to operate at full capacity with no extra seats. To fill those seats the airline may sell extra seating for a particular flight they have open space on, at a discounted rate. The airline will try their normal methods of booking so they may not make these seats available until the last minute. The best way that you can be prepared to take advantage of these extra sweet deals is to BE FLEXIBLE. Don't expect to get those deals on peak season and holidays. Expect to get the best priced seats midweek or on "red eye" seats late at night. But if you are willing to put up with these things you have a decent shot at saving some serious cash. When you go to lock on that flight, if you have a credit card that offers free flight insurance as a perk, you are that much better off.

TRY COMBO PACKAGES – Many airlines and travel web sites will offer combo rates on packages that include such things as rental car, hotel and airfare. If you need these other services, it is better to be able to get them at a discount and save additional money. Check several sites to see the best deal they can offer you. Some of the online travel sites to begin your search might be Kayak.com, Priceline.com, Hotwire.com and Expedia.com to name only a few.

LOOK AT SOME OF THE SMALLER REGIONAL AIRLINES – Some of the smaller regional airlines can offer some fantastic deals that can't be touched by some of the national chains. The reason they can do this is they don't have a vast amount of routes. The smaller regional will concentrate on highly popular destinations and try to make sure that they are able to fill as many seats on the plane as possible. An empty airline seat that could be filled even at a discount is lost revenue to an airline. Some of these regional carriers have smaller, non-stop flights to extremely popular destinations at inexpensive rates. These carriers work on the "buffet rule". The more people you serve, the less the cost per passenger. They try to make sure that every flight is full to capacity if possible. One of the leading regional airlines I have personally flown and enjoyed is called Allegiant Air.

Wikipedia has a list of other regional airlines in the U.S. and abroad. For that list, you can go to this link and see what you can save.

http://en.wikipedia.org/wiki/List_of_regional_airlines

INDIVIDUAL AIRLINE WEBSITES – In addition to the standard travel web sites, you can also check online or by phone with the individual airlines.

IF YOU HAVE ONE OF THOSE AIRLINE MILEAGE CREDIT CARDS, USE IT – If you do have one of those Airline Miles cards see if you have sufficient miles to get a free or discounted ticket. You have to use your head though, if you have two airlines offering the same destination and in order to get the free miles you have to use a more expensive airline to get the miles, is it worth the extra cost? Is that actually going to help you? Use your head and read the fine print. Always compare all of your options. Only spend money if it makes sense and you can afford it.

HOTELS, MOTELS AND VACATION DESTINATIONS WHY WOULD A HOTEL OR MOTEL OFFER A DISCOUNT – For the precise reason that the airlines do. Hotels and motels are owned by savvy business people. These folks know that there is a certain amount of expenses that need to be covered just to have their hotel or motel open, regardless of how many customers are staying there. This is called an "Occupancy Rate". Occupancy Rates vary by the hotel as well as time of the week and season. For instance, most hotels have a higher occupancy rate on Friday and Saturday nights because more people are seeking to stay over the weekend. This also means it's harder to find a terrific deal on a hotel room on Friday or Saturday.

If the hotel has an 80% occupancy rate, this means that on an average, only 80% of their rooms are being rented out and an empty hotel room makes them no money. It makes sense as a business person to pull out all stops to rent those empty rooms even at a slight discount. As an example, have you ever had a pre-set reservation at a hotel and go by their sign or marquee out front and it says,"VACANCY - Rooms from $49.99 and up." You might have a reservation for $69.00 at the same hotel (if this is the case I always ask for the discounted rate and most hotels will oblige or tell you what the difference in the room that you are paying for is). They are trying to rent out the vacant hotel rooms to spur of the moment at a discounted price to help cover expenses and make another happy customer that might spread the word about their facility. A full hotel room makes them some money and is better for their bottom line. In addition they have an opportunity to make additional money on dining, drinks, in room movies, etc. It might not make as much profit as the published rates, but it surely does help some in the overall budget. Why not take advantage of this opportunity and help out your budget?

ONLINE DISCOUNT HOTEL WEBSITES – I don't want to be redundant here. The same thing applies, and the same sites as I listed above under airfare. The discount travel sites work just as well for discounted hotels. Some of the discounted travel sites to begin your search would be Kayak.com, Priceline.com, Hotwire.com and Expedia.com among others.

USE YOUR DISCOUNTS – By being part of a large group such as AAA (Automobile Association of America – Road Service Plan) or AARP (American Association of Retired Persons) many hotels and motels will give a discount if you show them your membership card. One other discount to ask for is if you live in the local state or area and are just taking a little time to relax, ask the person at the front desk if they offer "local discounts". What better way to get the local people to come and relax and fill a few rooms while they are at it. In addition if you are over the age of sixty five you can always ask if a motel, restaurant, attraction or movie theatre offers senior citizen discount. Let that grey hair earn you a discount. You earned it!

TRAVELING & ON THE ROAD TIPS

OFF THE BEATEN PATH - Some of the best food and memories that our family made when traveling were because we asked local people we came into contact with where they went to eat and where they went to have an enjoyable time when they were not working. Think about yourself and the people you know. You probably know the best places in town to eat and those particular spots that are popular for the locals, like that secret swimming hole that everyone congregates or some other secret spot that is unique to your area.

When you are traveling, take the time to ask the person behind the counter in a restaurant or hotel where THEY go and what they do when they are not working for fun. Ask for the things that are off the beaten path. You will be amazed at the outstanding memories you will enjoy from the golden tips that these folks will share with you. Always remember to be courteous and ask people. Most will be happy to share.

SPECIAL DISCOUNTS & TIME SHARES –

LOCAL DISCOUNTS – If you live in a high tourist area and you are a local resident, did you know that many tourist attractions and local businesses offer deep discounts to locals? Just call or ask the business if they offer discounts to local residents. You may have to show your local driver's license or I.D. as proof of local residency, but the savings can be immense. Remember these businesses have an active interest in bringing the locals to their businesses since the tourist trade usually runs in cycles depending on the time of the year that you are dealing with. If you know of any outstanding discounts that are offered in your area that you want people to know about, please send them to my email so I can update in future editions. My email address is georgerburke@yahoo.com.

ANNUAL PASS – Many local tourist attractions, amusement parks, museums, zoos, aquariums and botanical gardens offer a highly discounted annual pass. If you live close by, and feel that you will use the pass it might save you a substantial amount of money. Usually these passes are equal to the cost of what only a couple of daily passes would cost you. When considering these plans see if they include parking as that can be an expensive add on.

RECIPROCAL AGREEMENTS – Are you ready to hit the road and have some fun? Do you have an annual pass at an aquarium or zoo from your local area? Did you know that many zoos, aquariums, museums and botanical gardens have reciprocal agreements? This means that if you have an annual pass to the one in your local area, they may have an agreement to allow annual pass holders from across the nation at other like places free or discounted access to their facility and Visa Versa. This means that you may go to these other zoos, aquariums, museums or botanical gardens for free or at the highly discounted daily rates that their members enjoy. Call your local zoo, aquarium, museum or botanical garden or visit their web site and see what other places they have a reciprocal agreement with and enjoy the savings!

http://www.aza.org/education/kidsandfamilies/detail.aspx?id=264

As the Author, I am always happy to hear from you, the readers.

TO REVIEW THE BOOK:

Please go to Amazon.com and leave feedback on the Amazon Page for this book – Financial Cents – How To Survive In A High Dollar World. You can also mark "Like" if you found this information helpful. I am always happy to hear from you. I read all Reviews left on the page and welcome you to leave your honest opinion.

TO CONTACT THE AUTHOR

Please feel free to email me your ideas or money saving tips you would be interested in sharing with our readers in updates to this book for all to benefit from. You can email me at:

georgerburke@yahoo.com

LOOK FOR MY UPCOMING YOUTUBE MONEY SAVING TIPS CHANNEL. **FINANCIAL CENTS**

www.ingramcontent.com/pod-product-compliance
Lightning Source LLC
Chambersburg PA
CBHW061515180526
45171CB00001B/188